This book belongs to

....

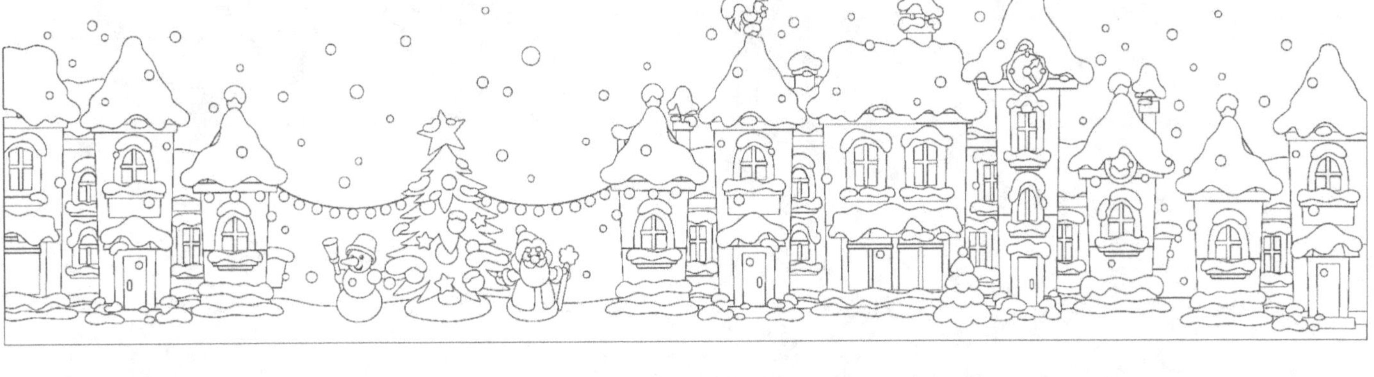

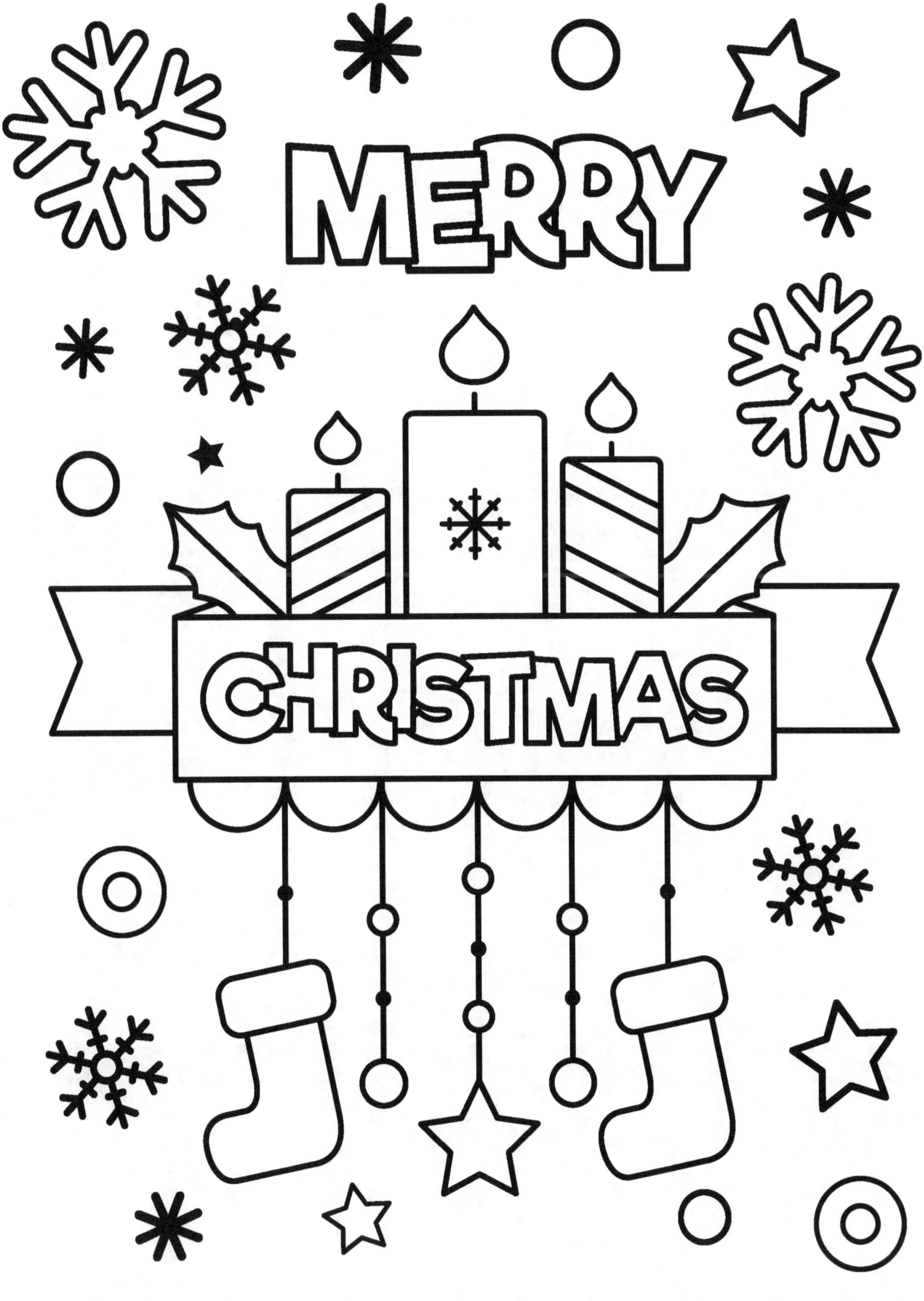
MERRY
CHRISTMAS

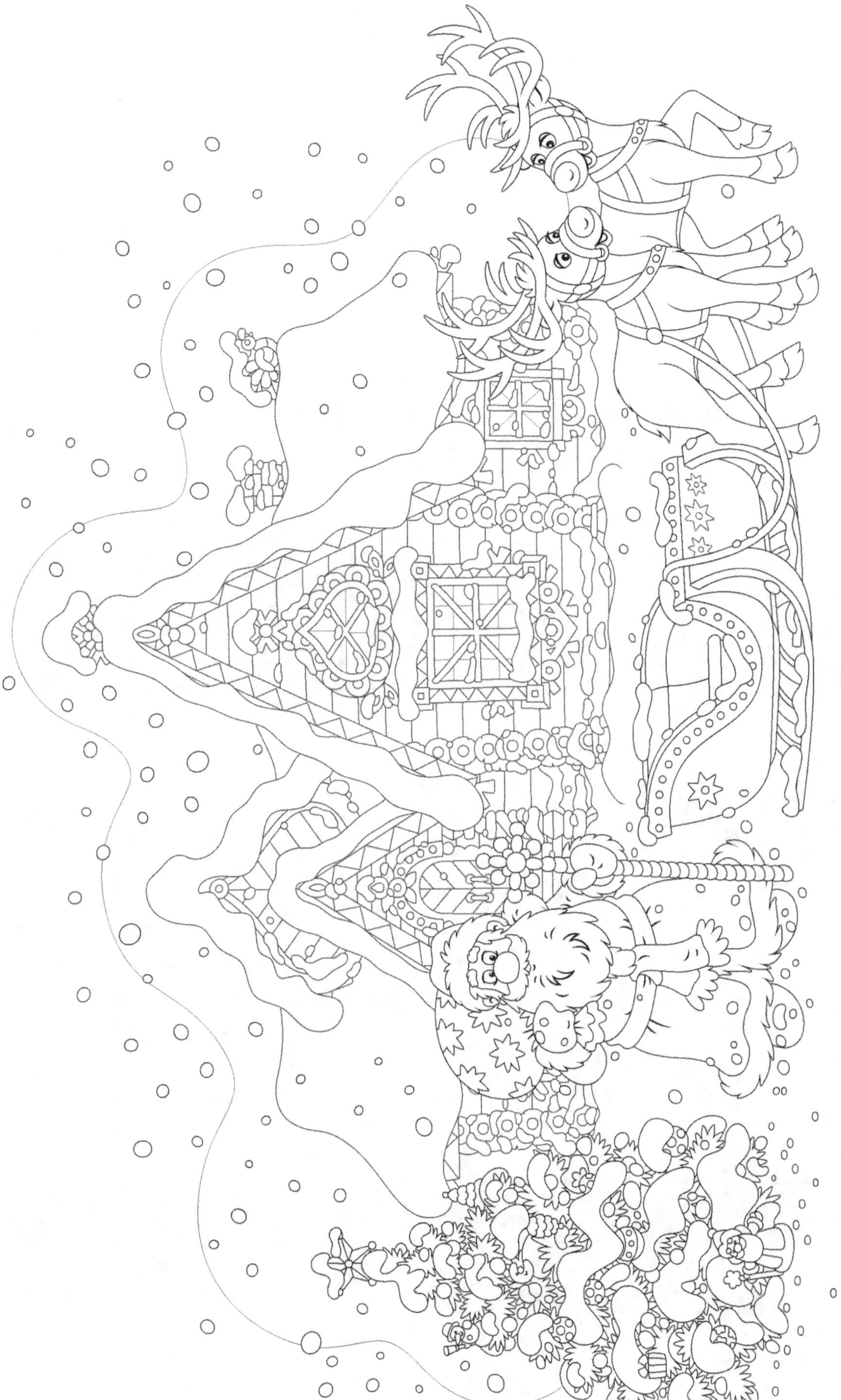

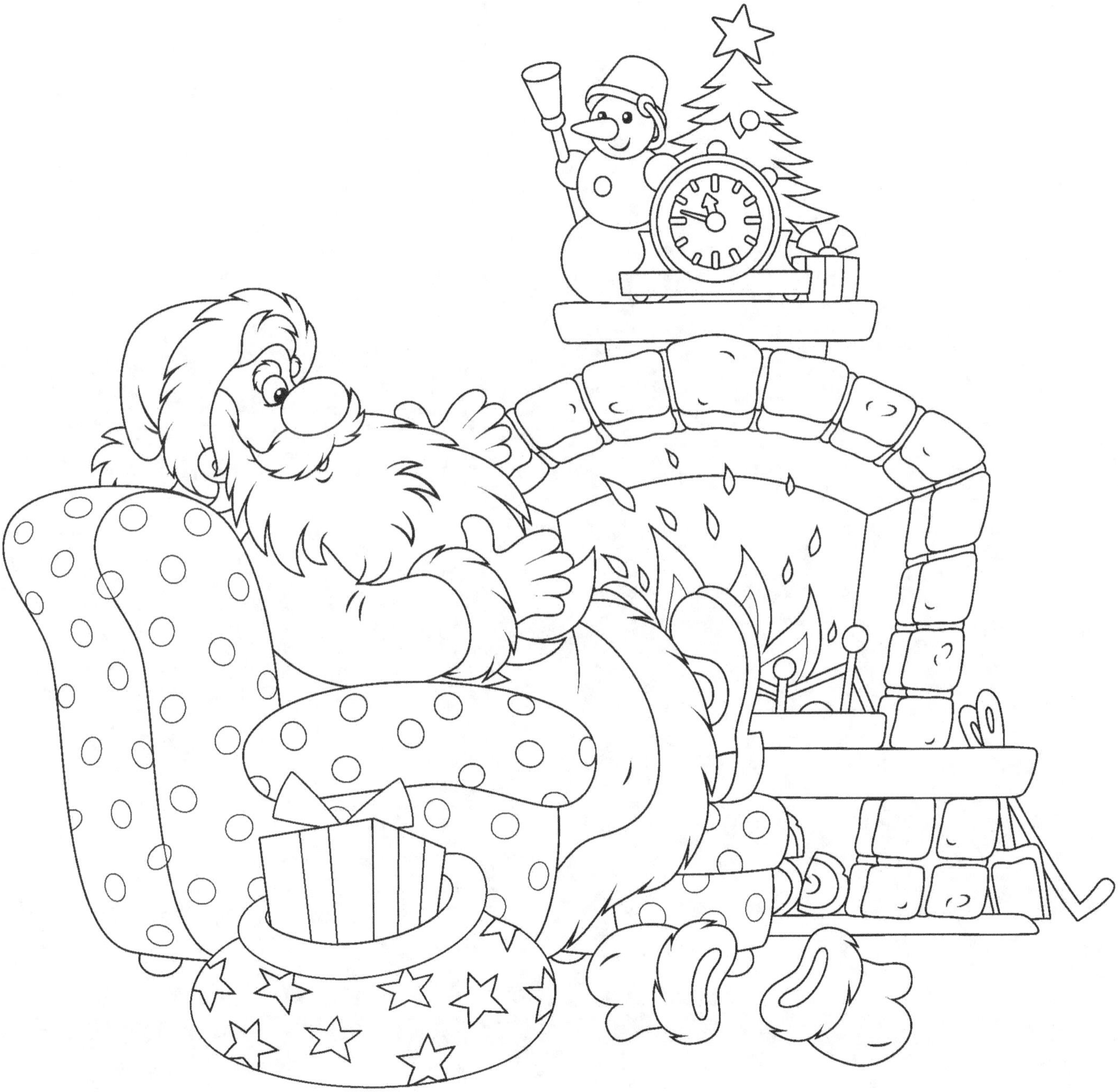

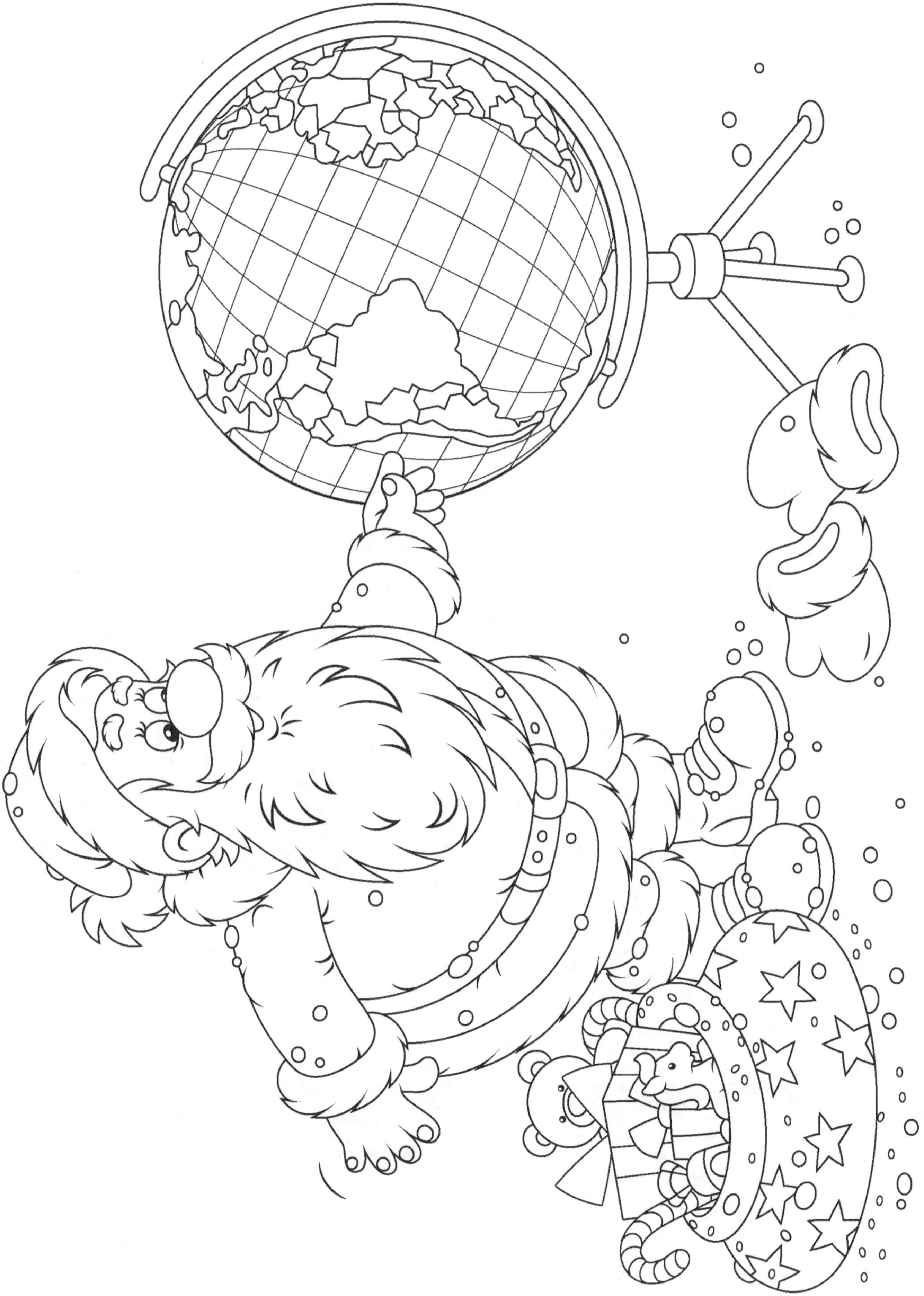

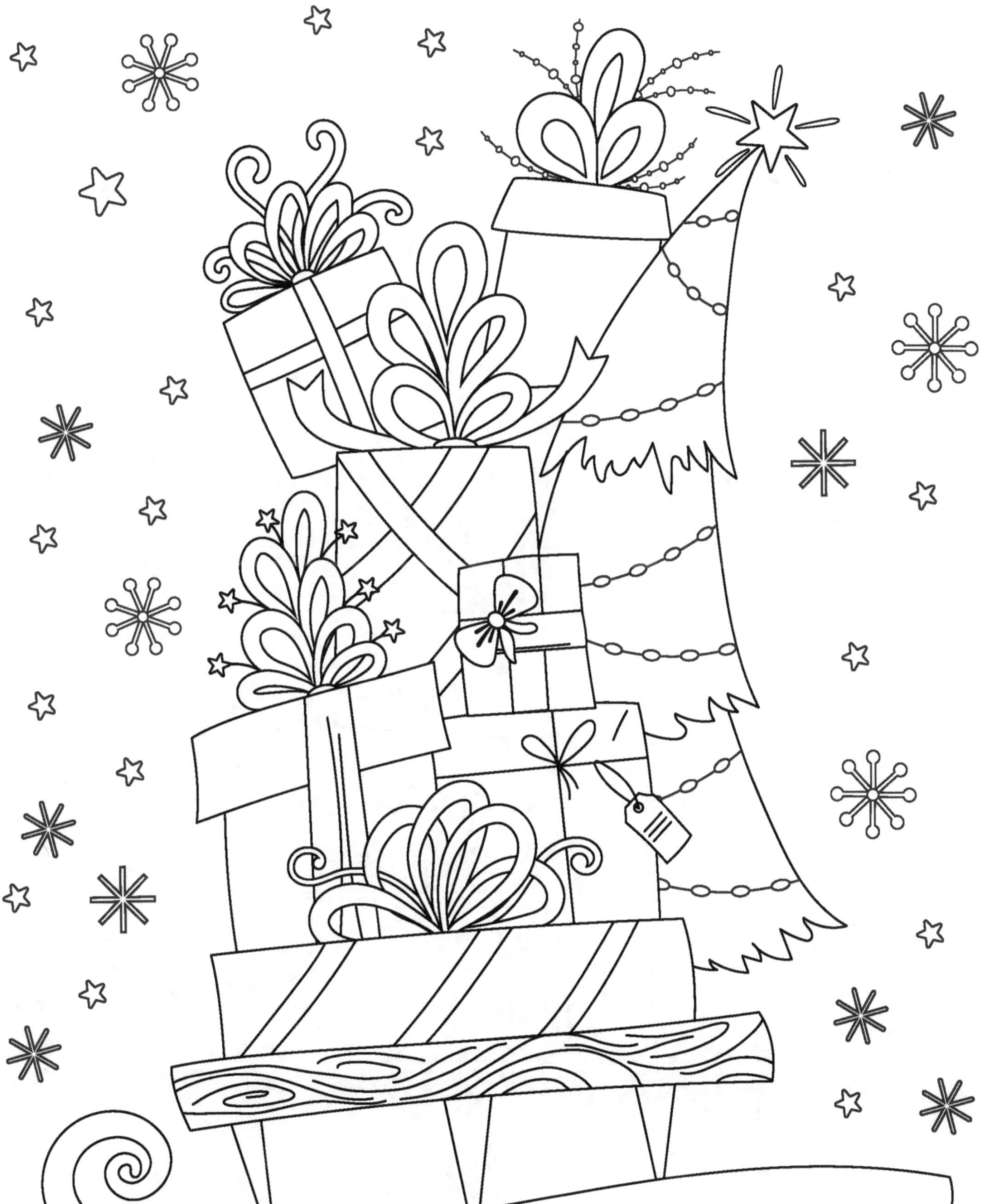

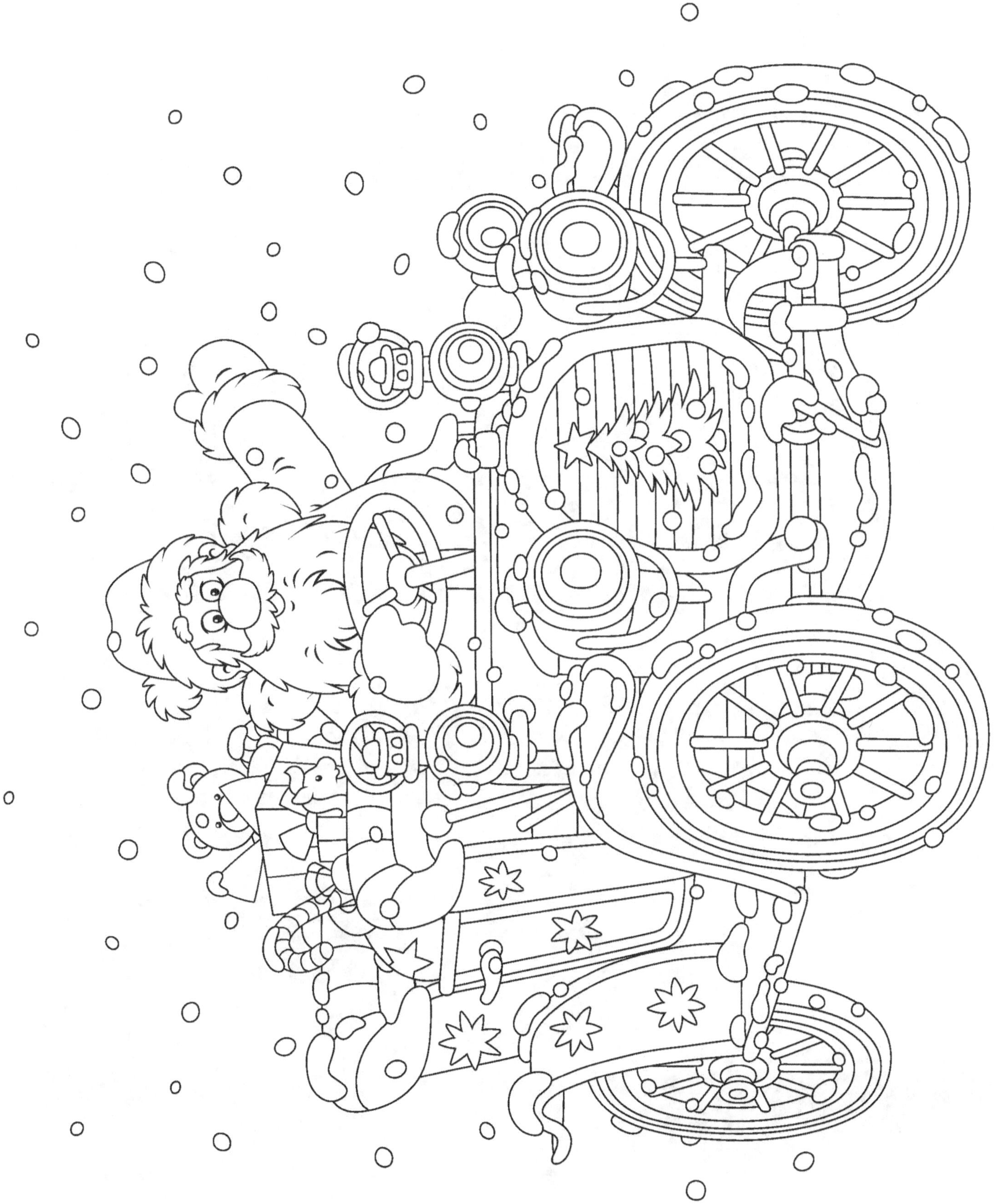

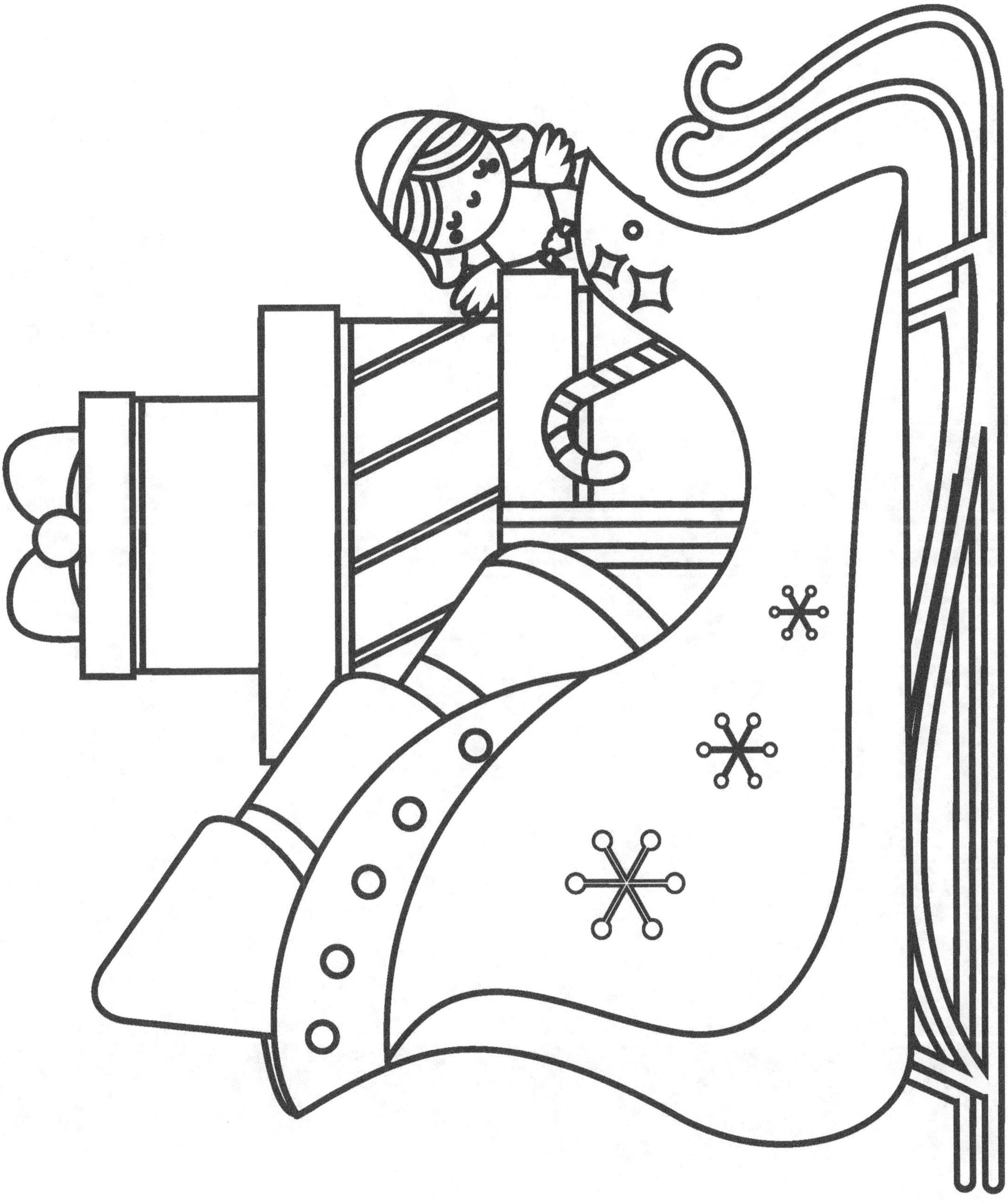

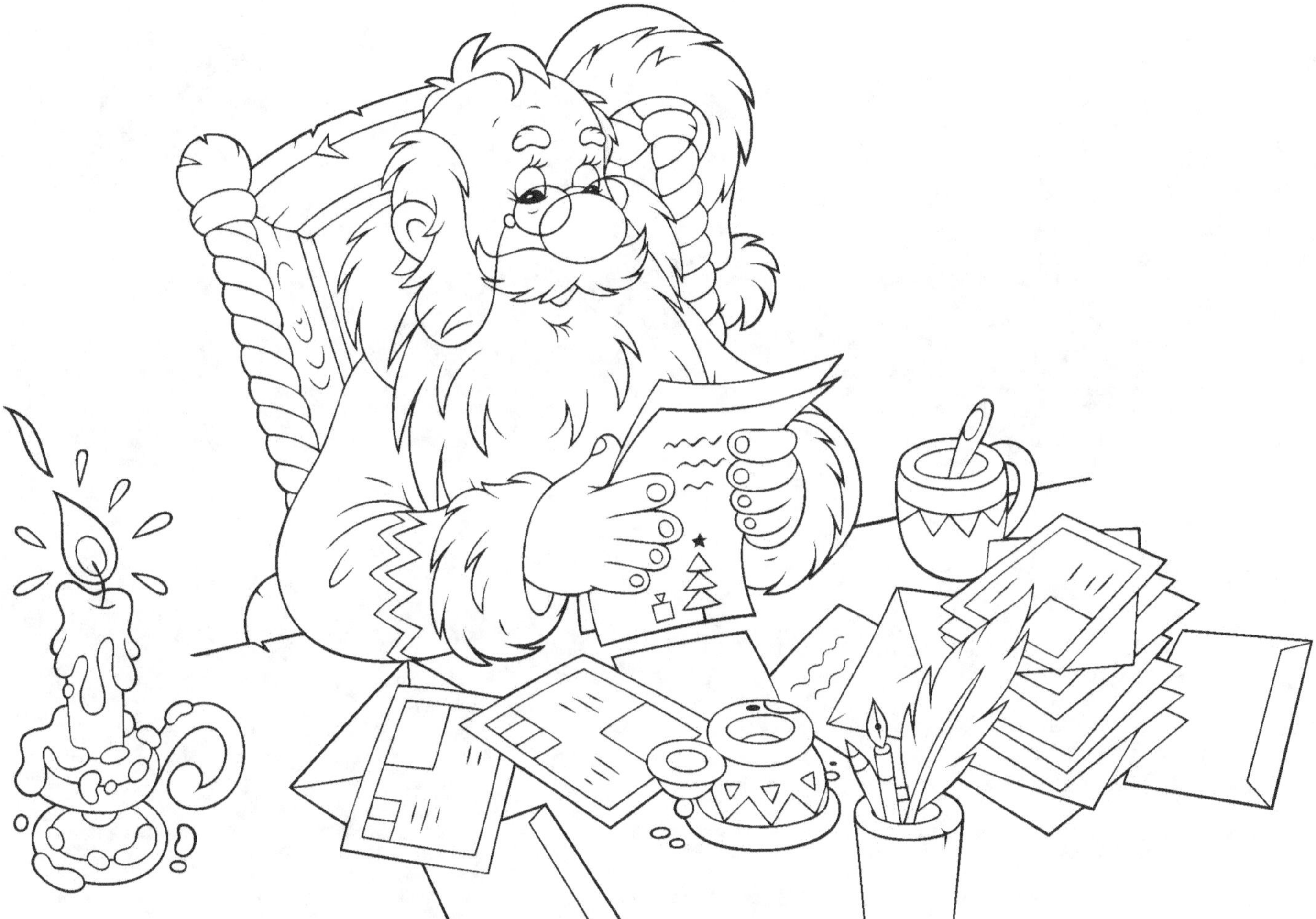

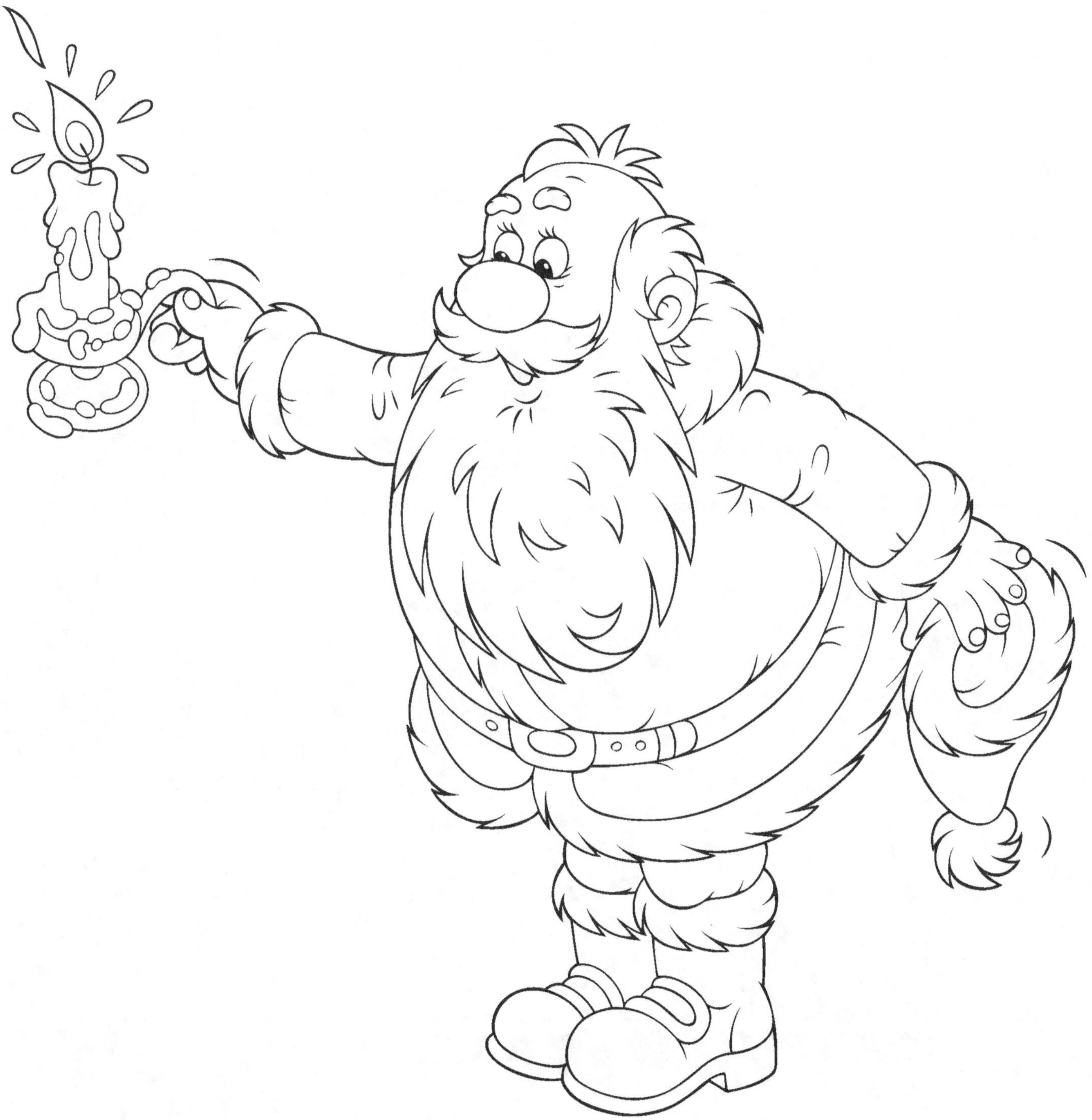

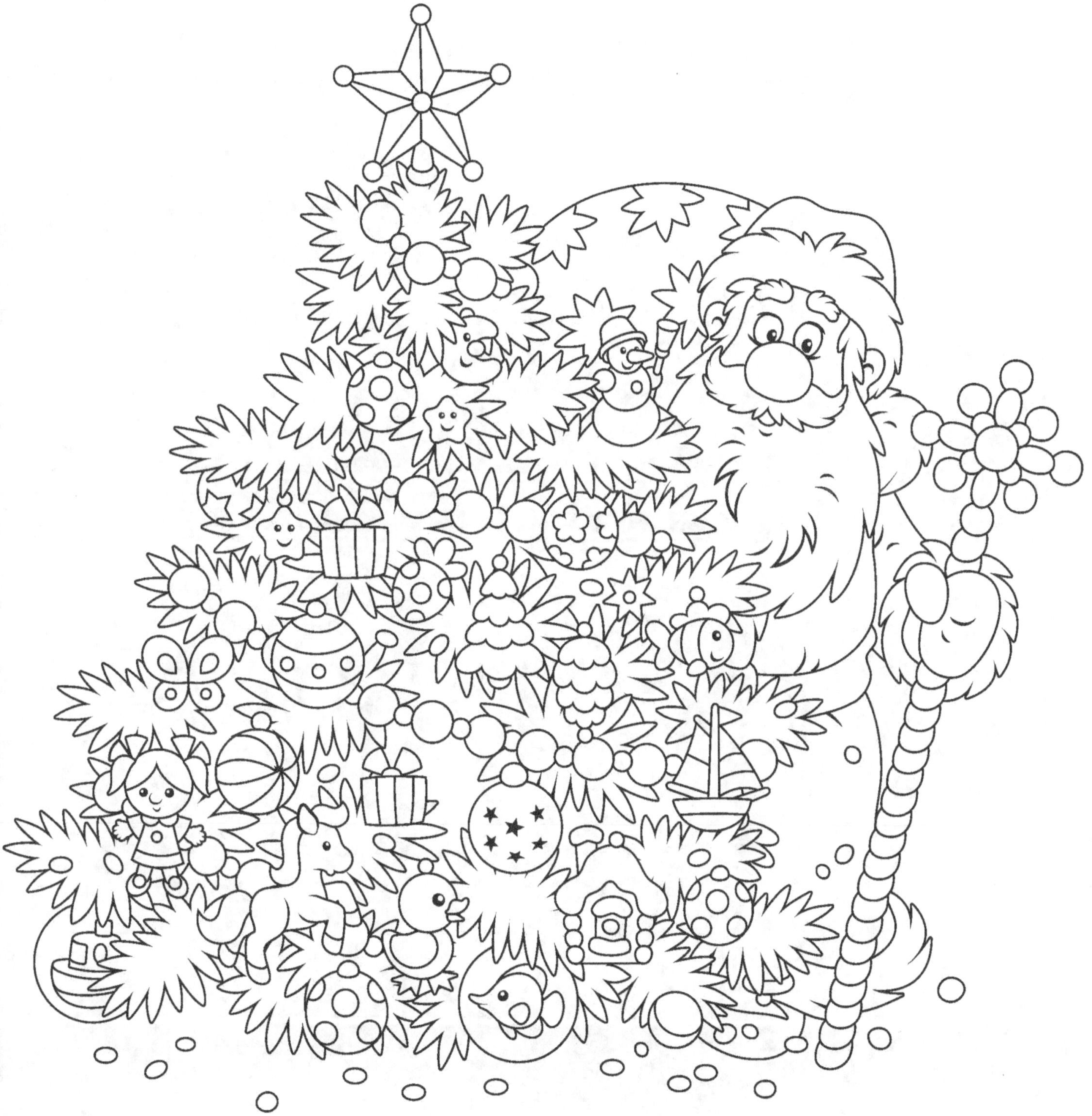

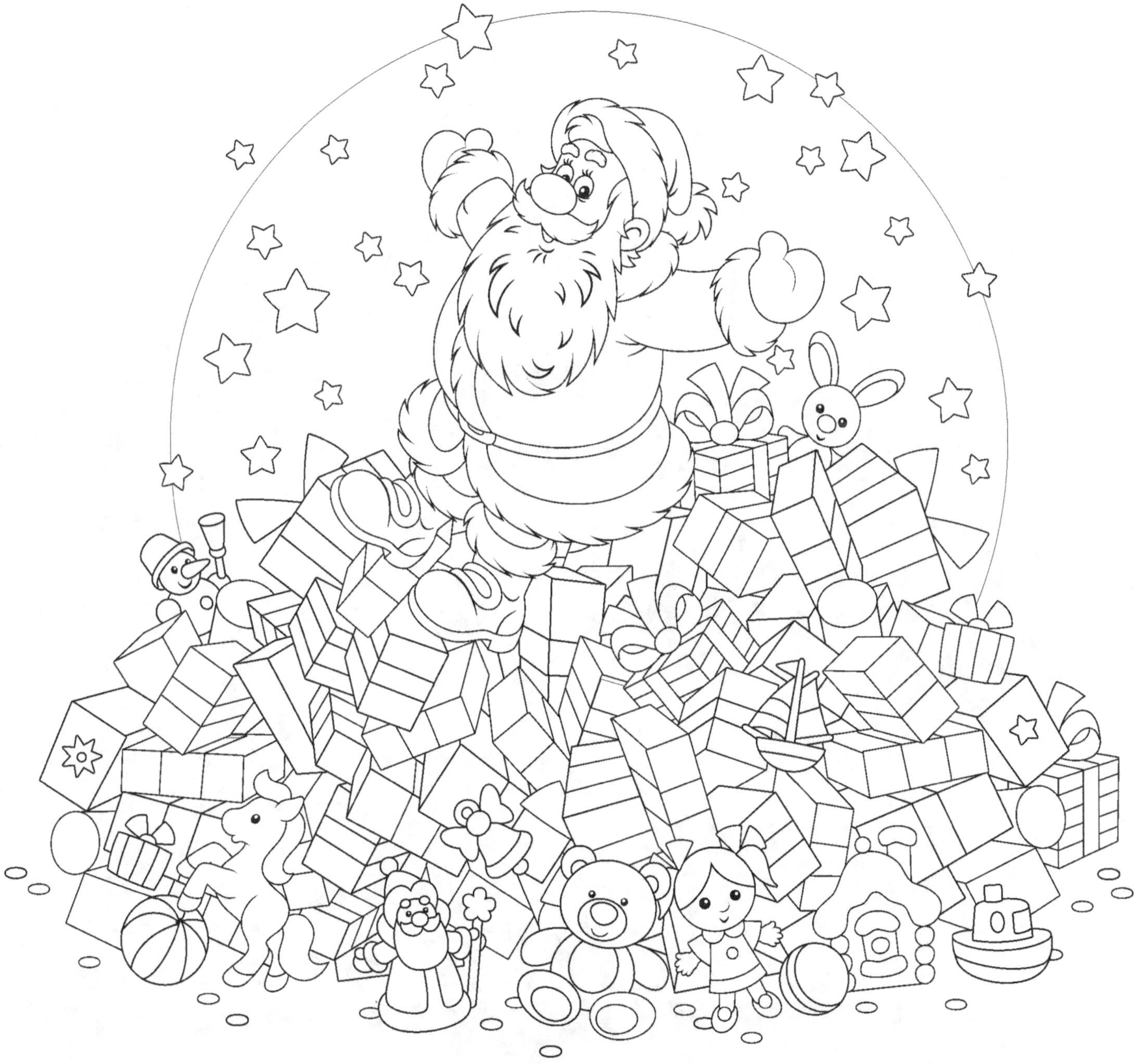

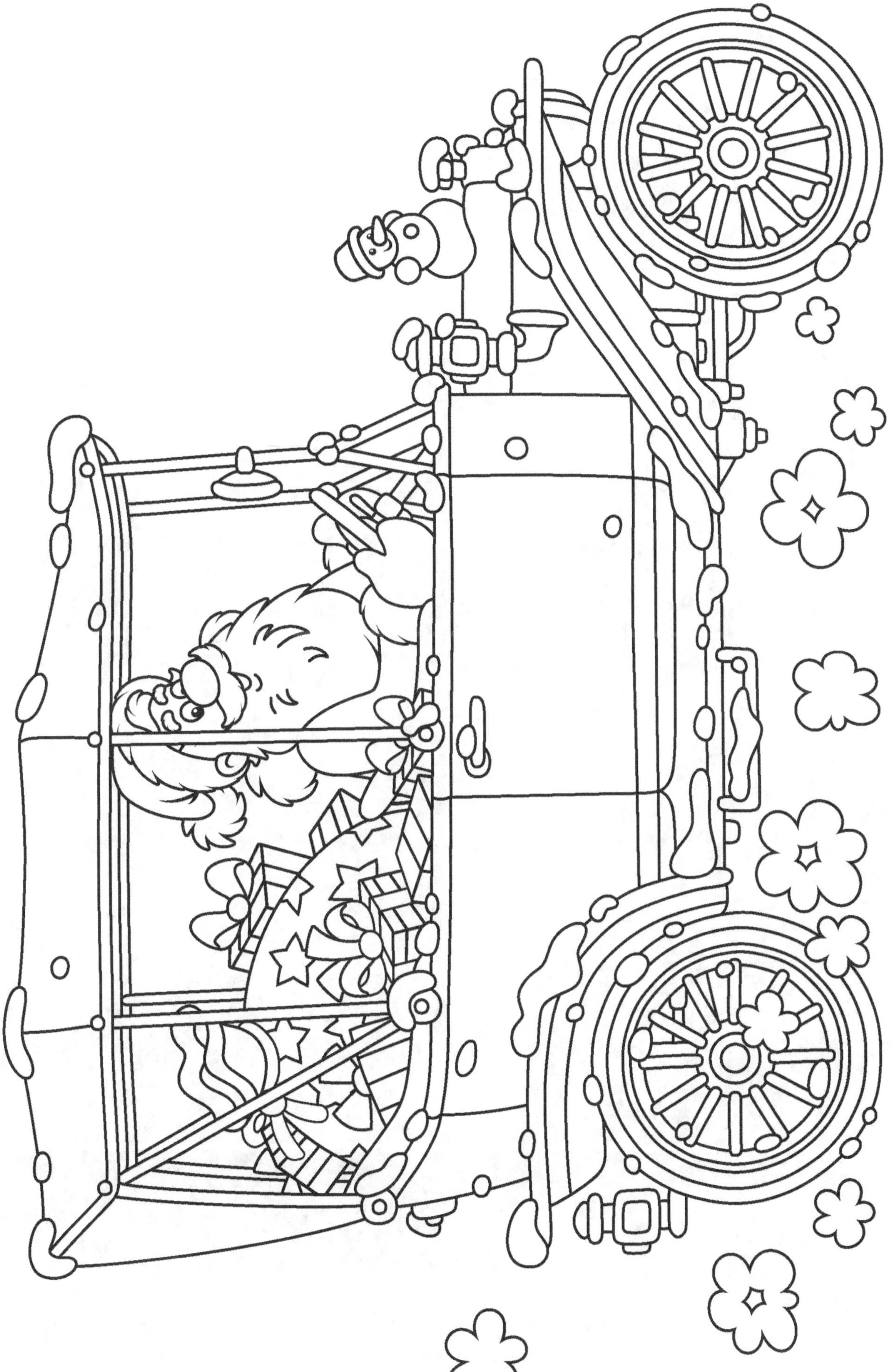

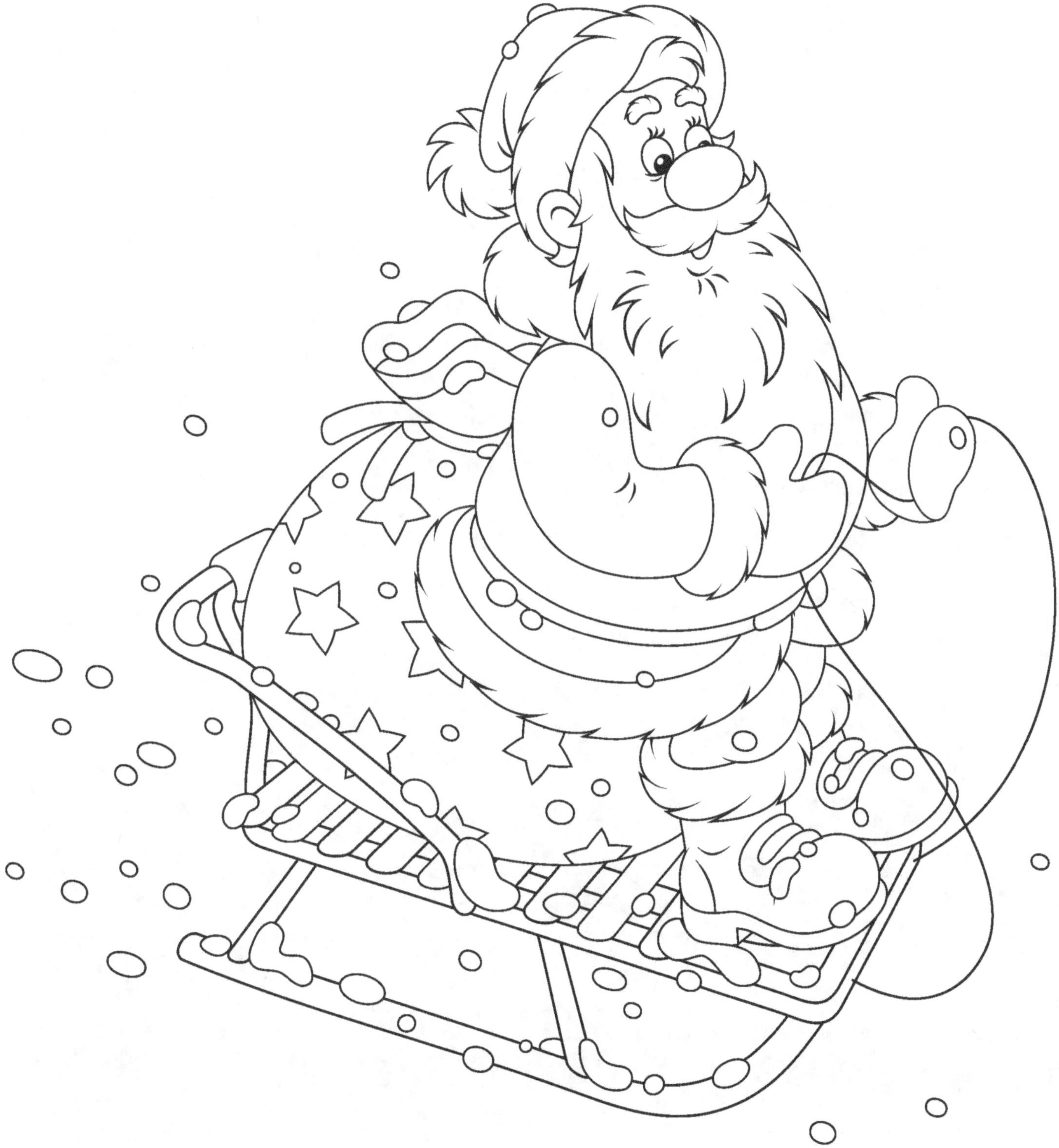

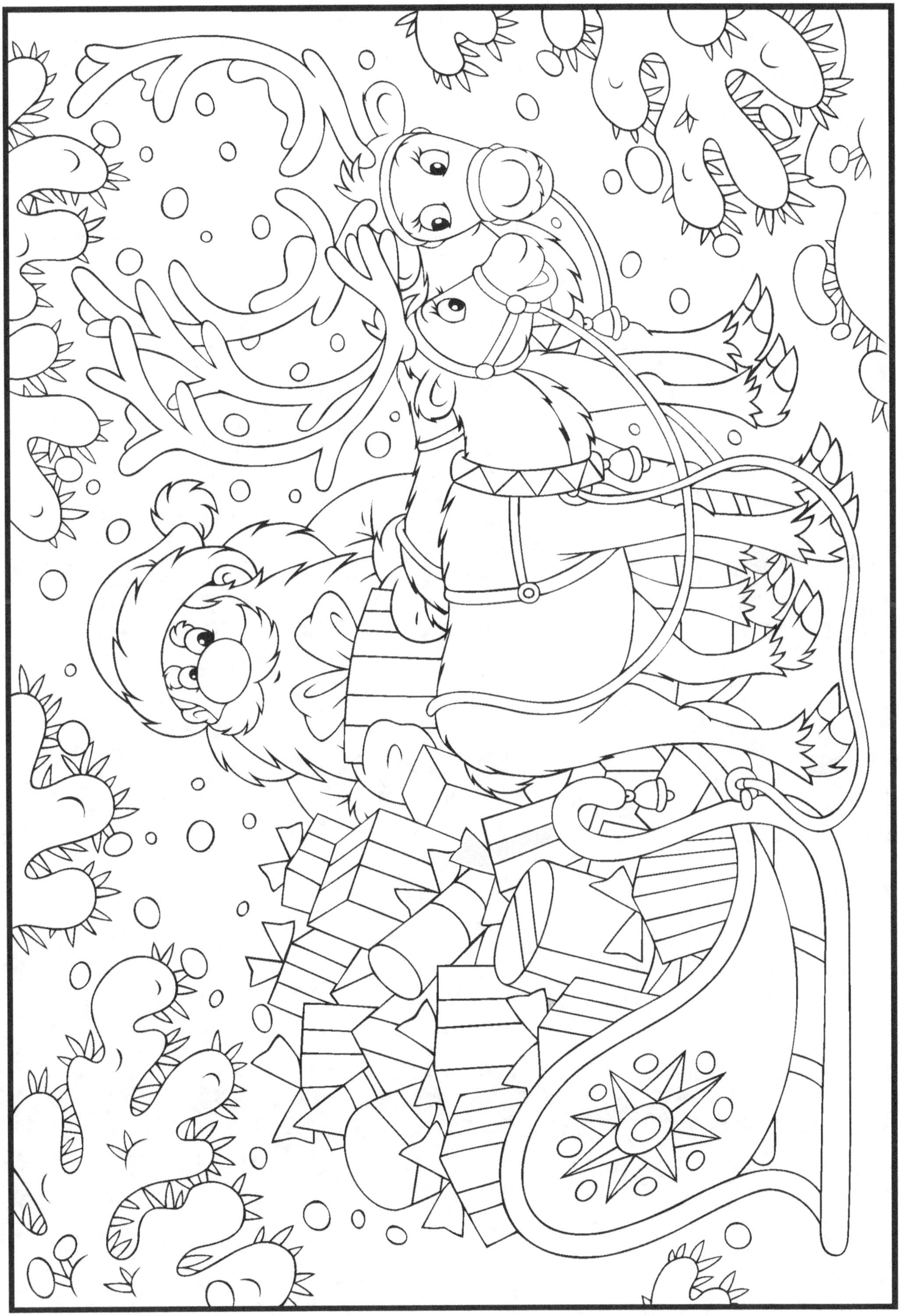

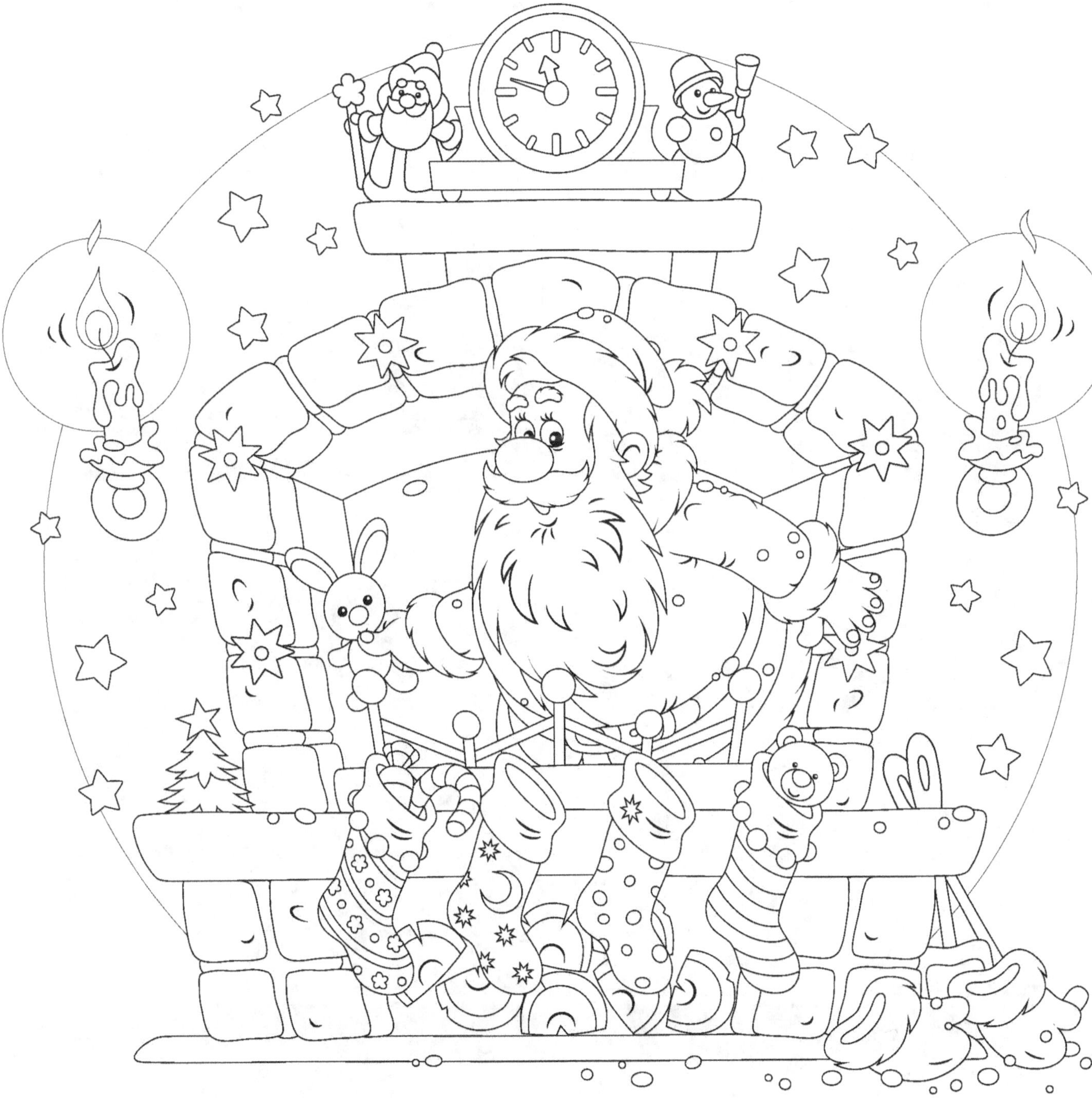

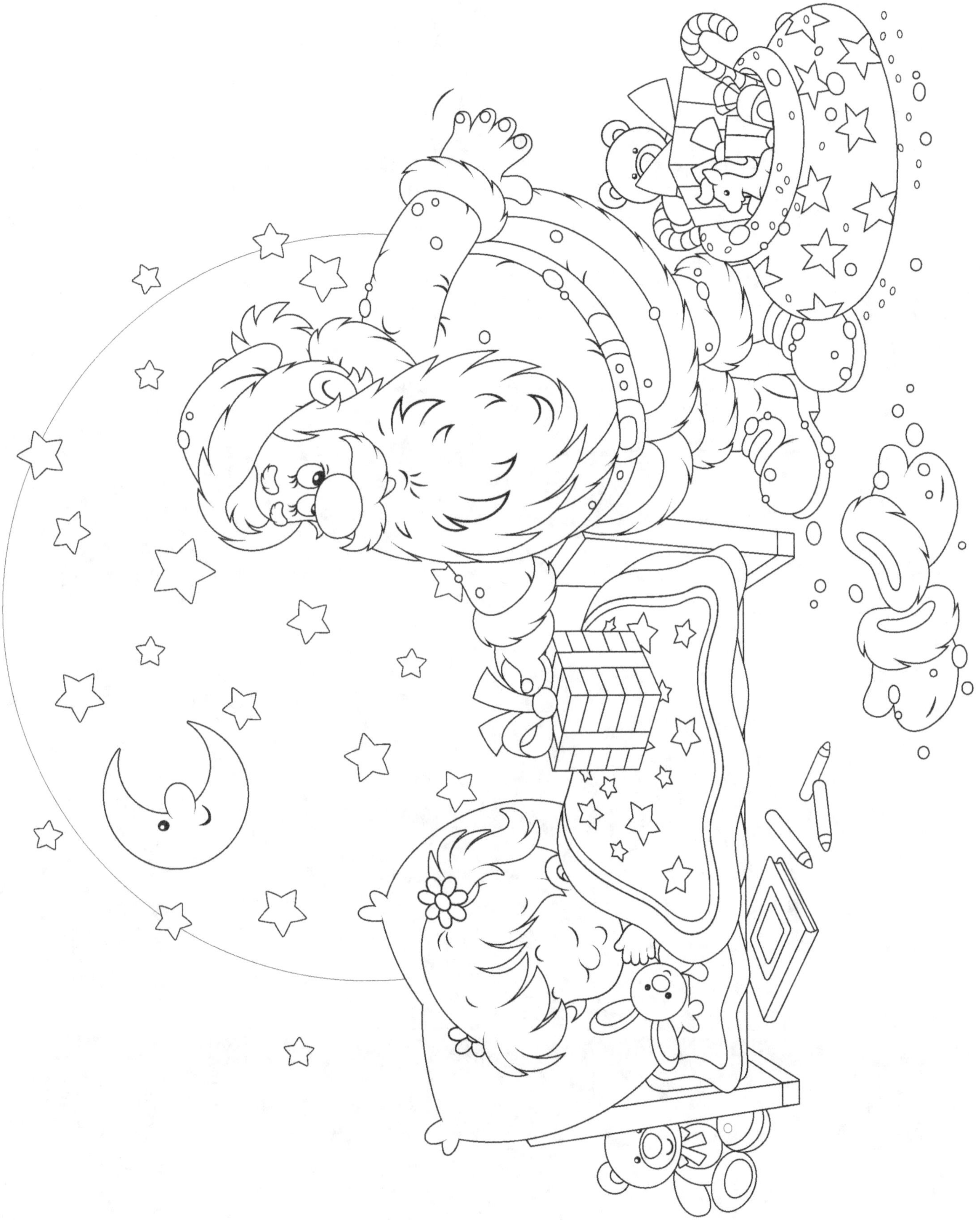

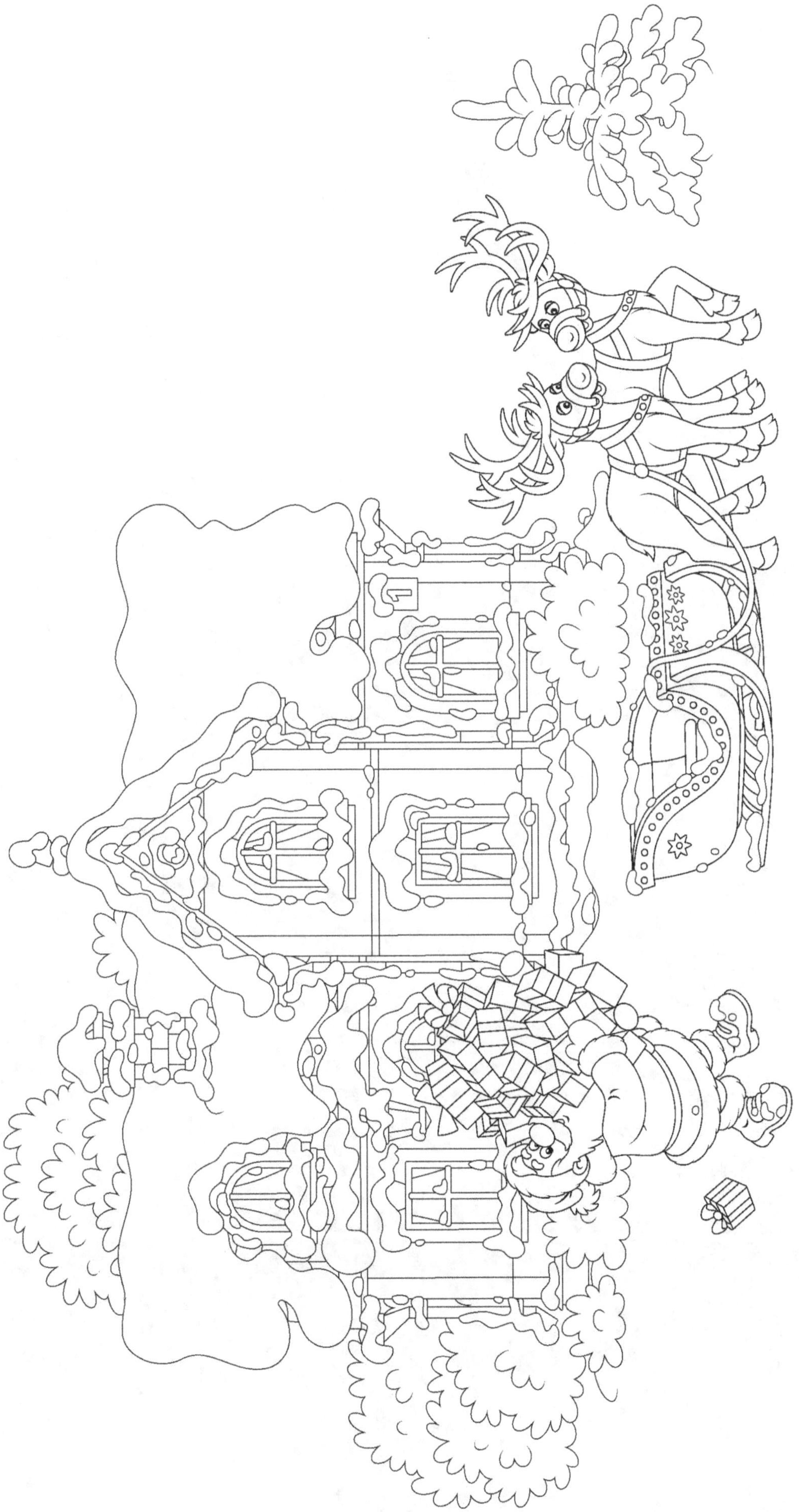

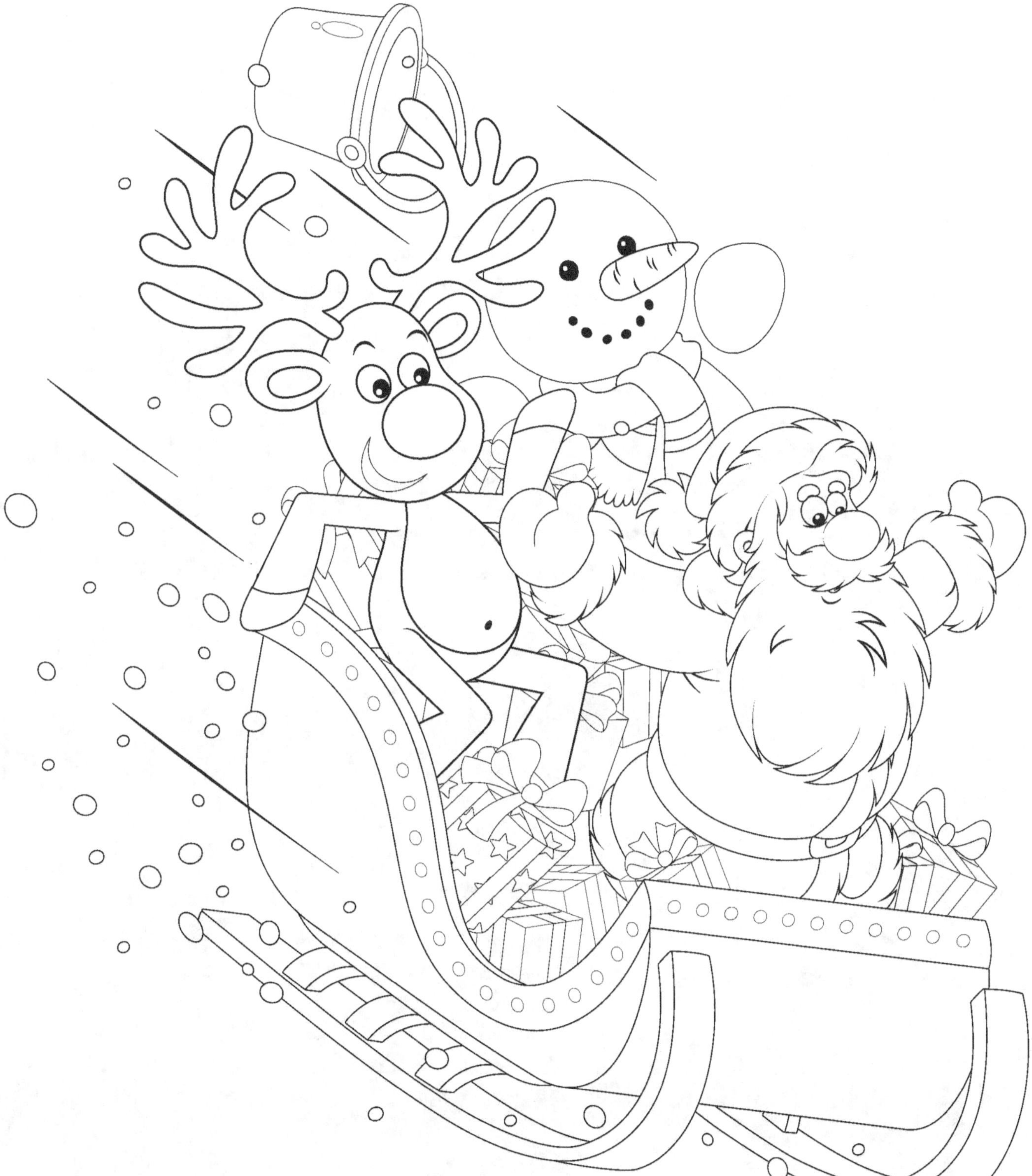

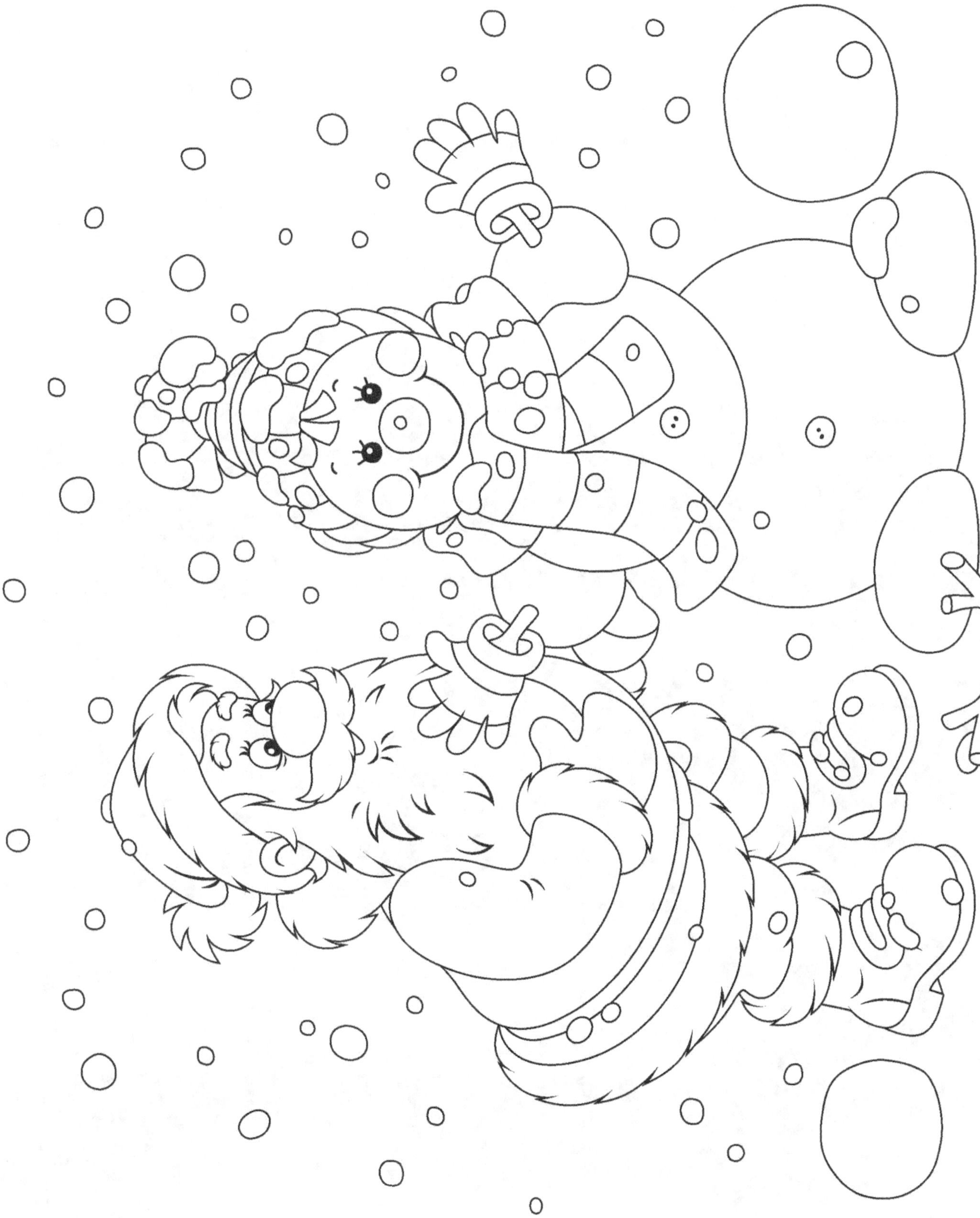

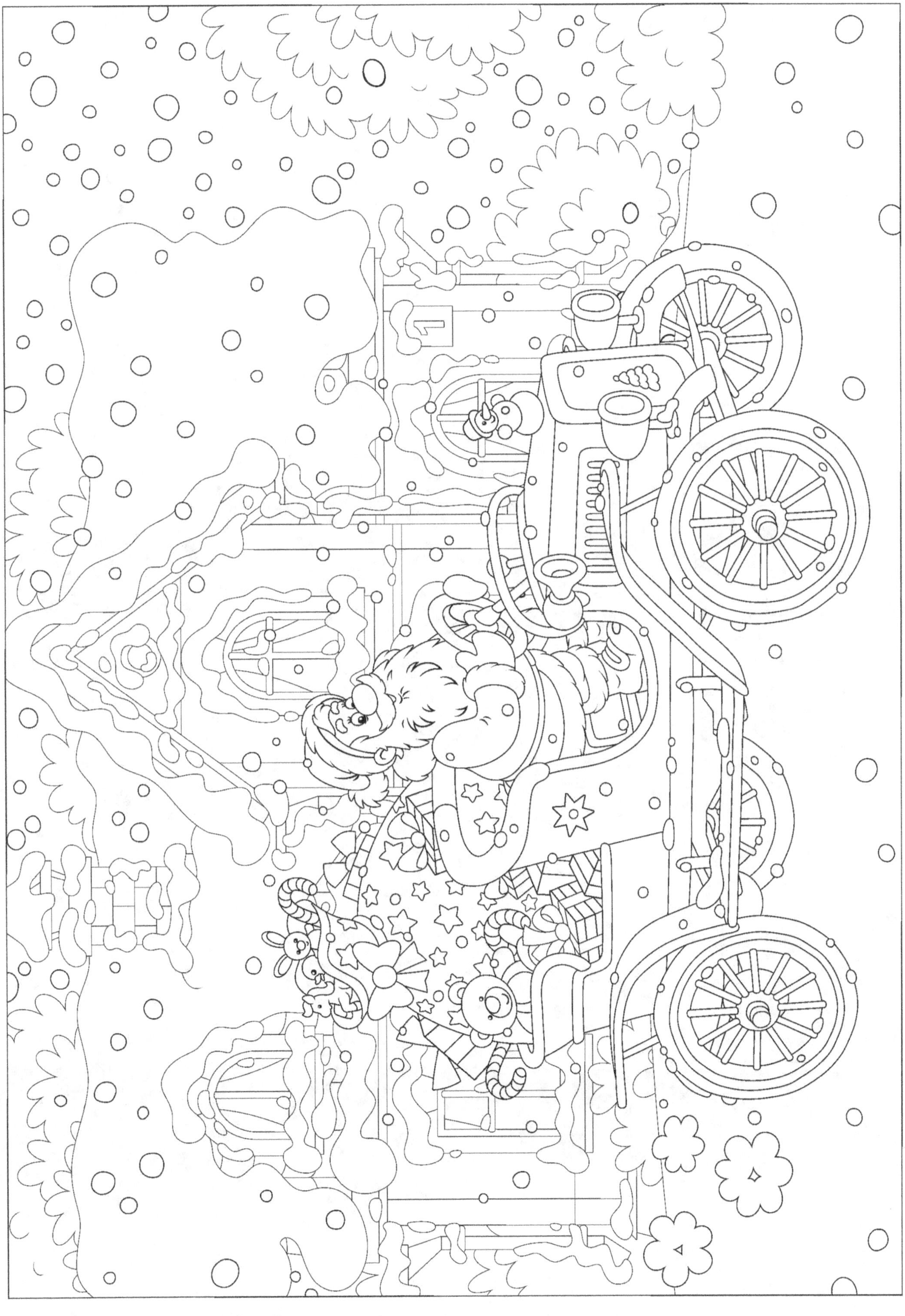

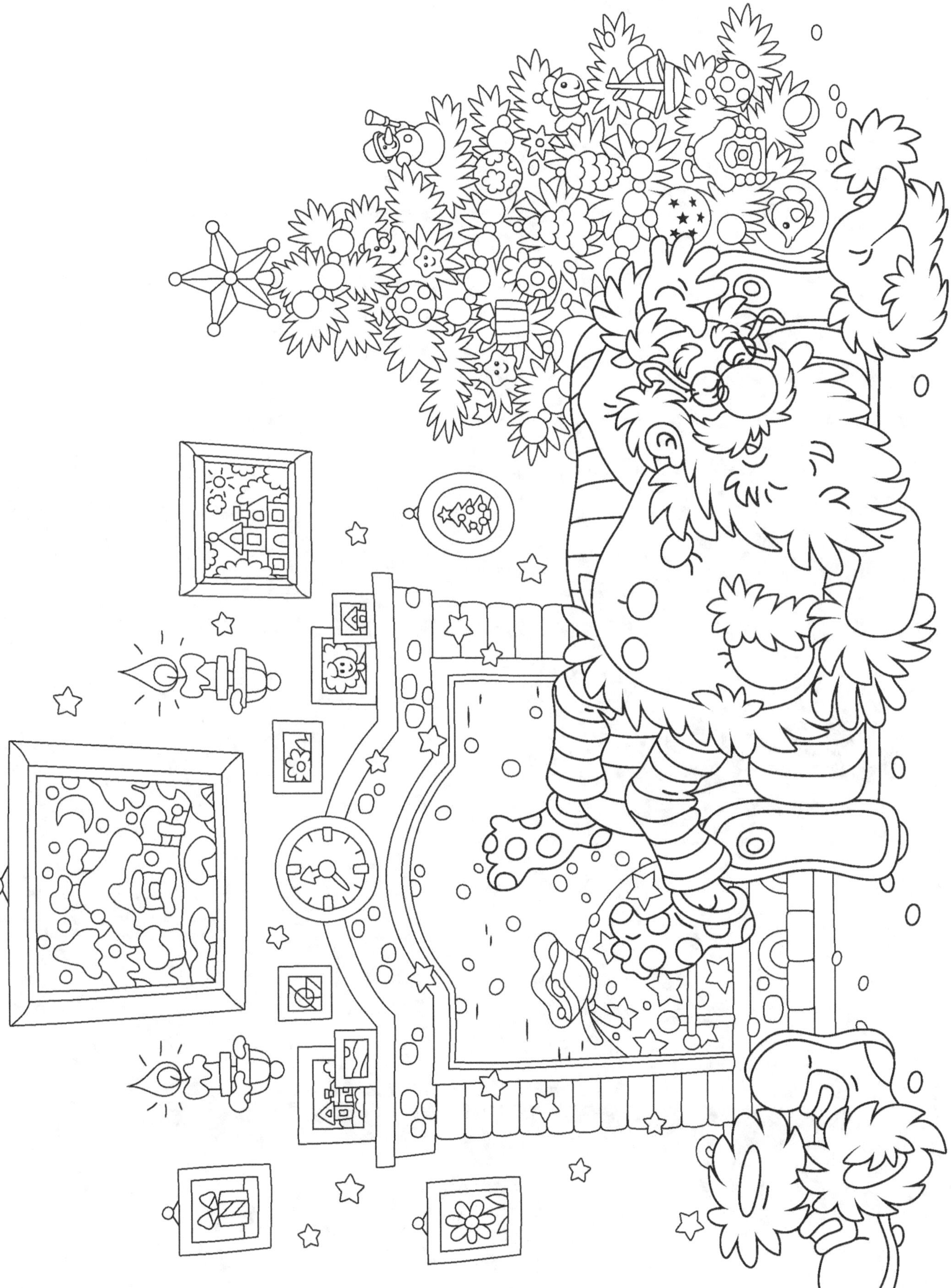

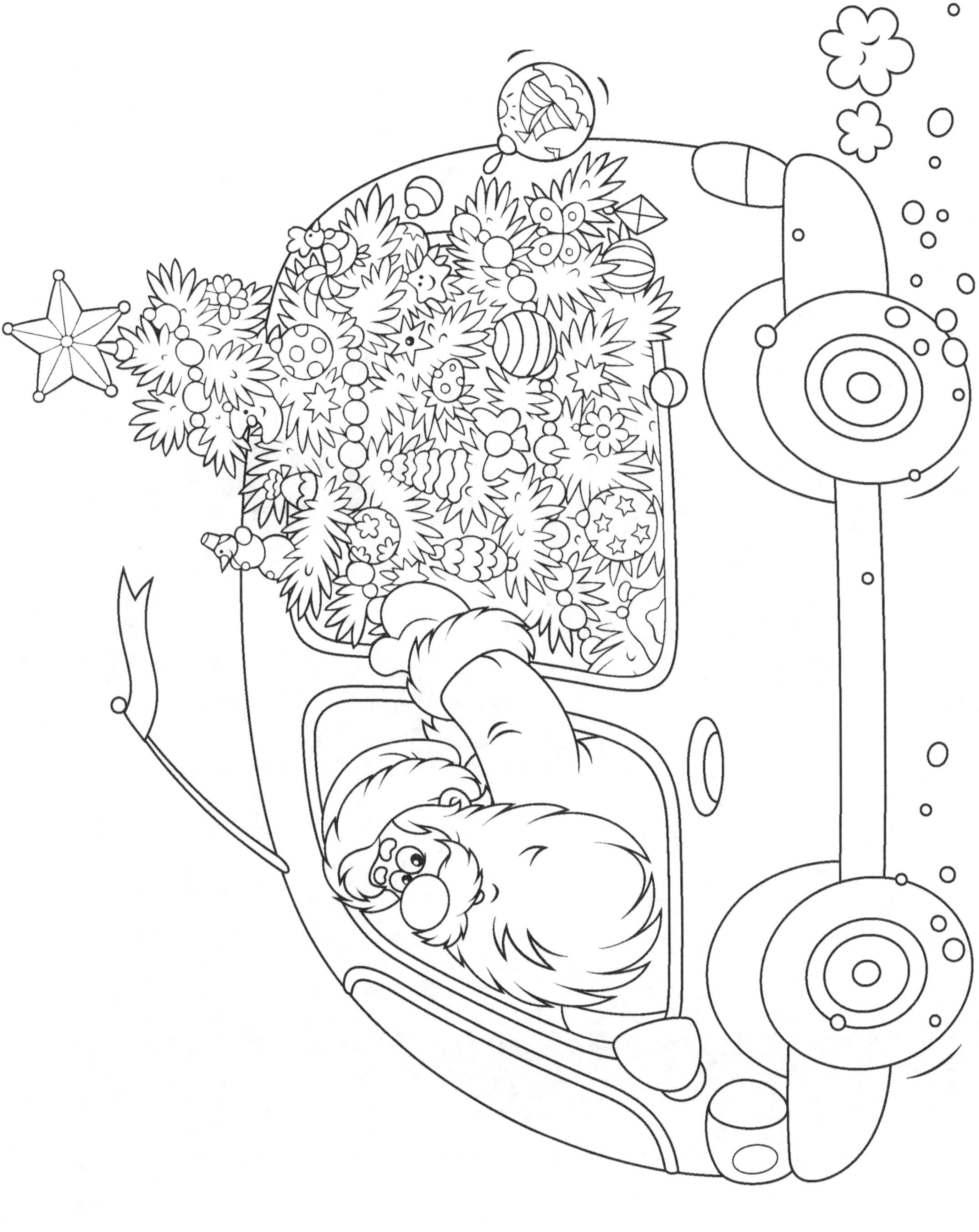

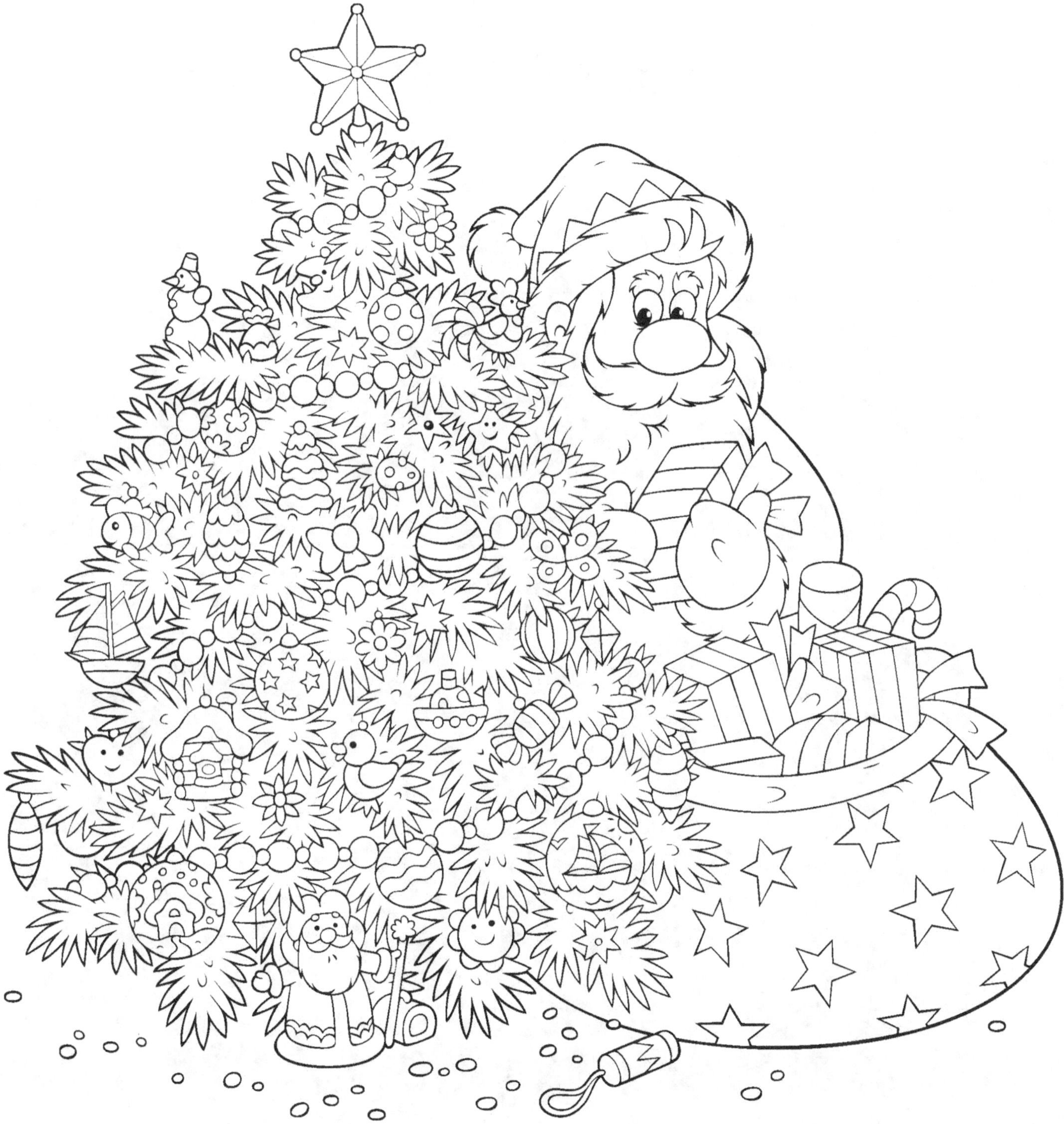

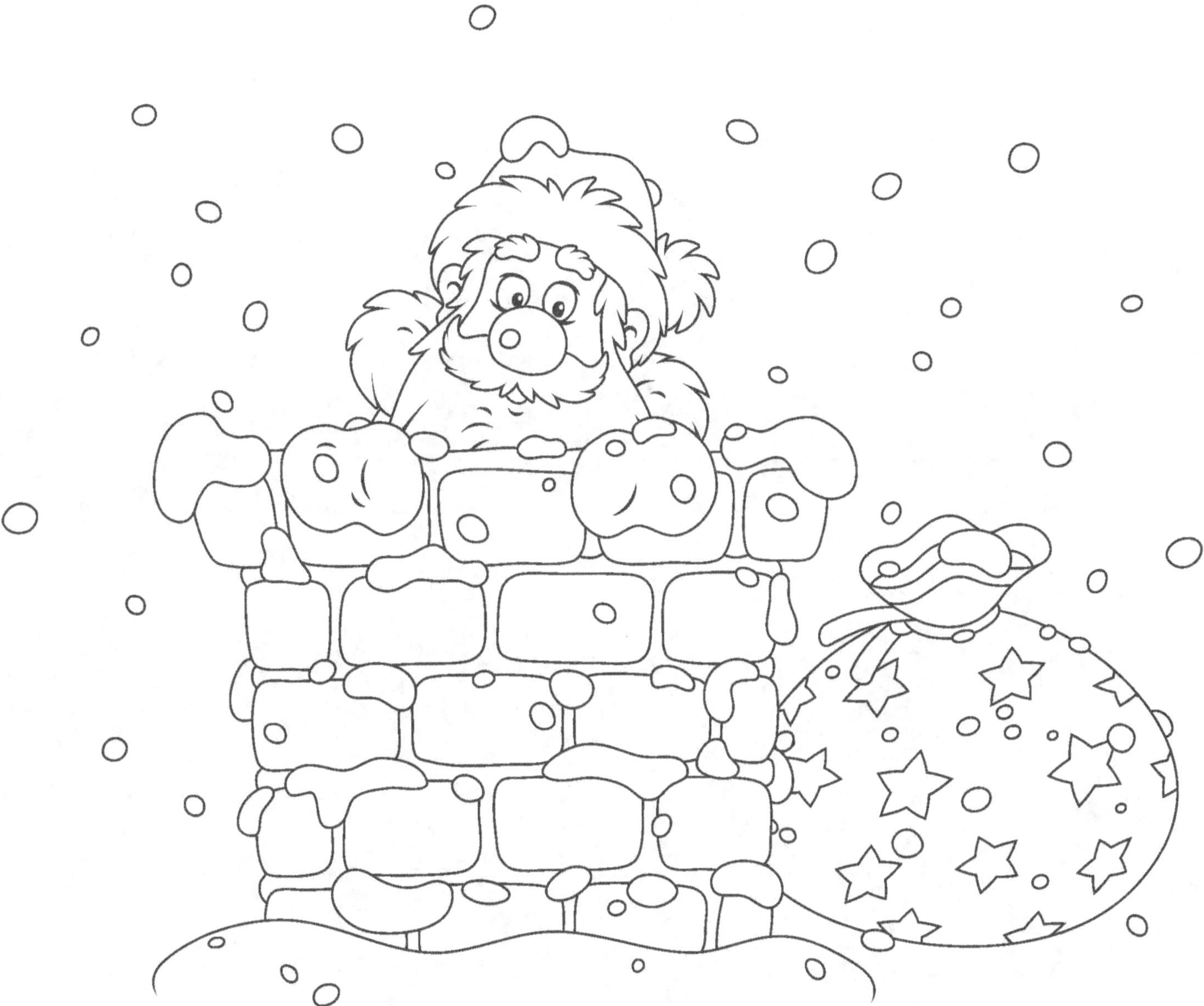

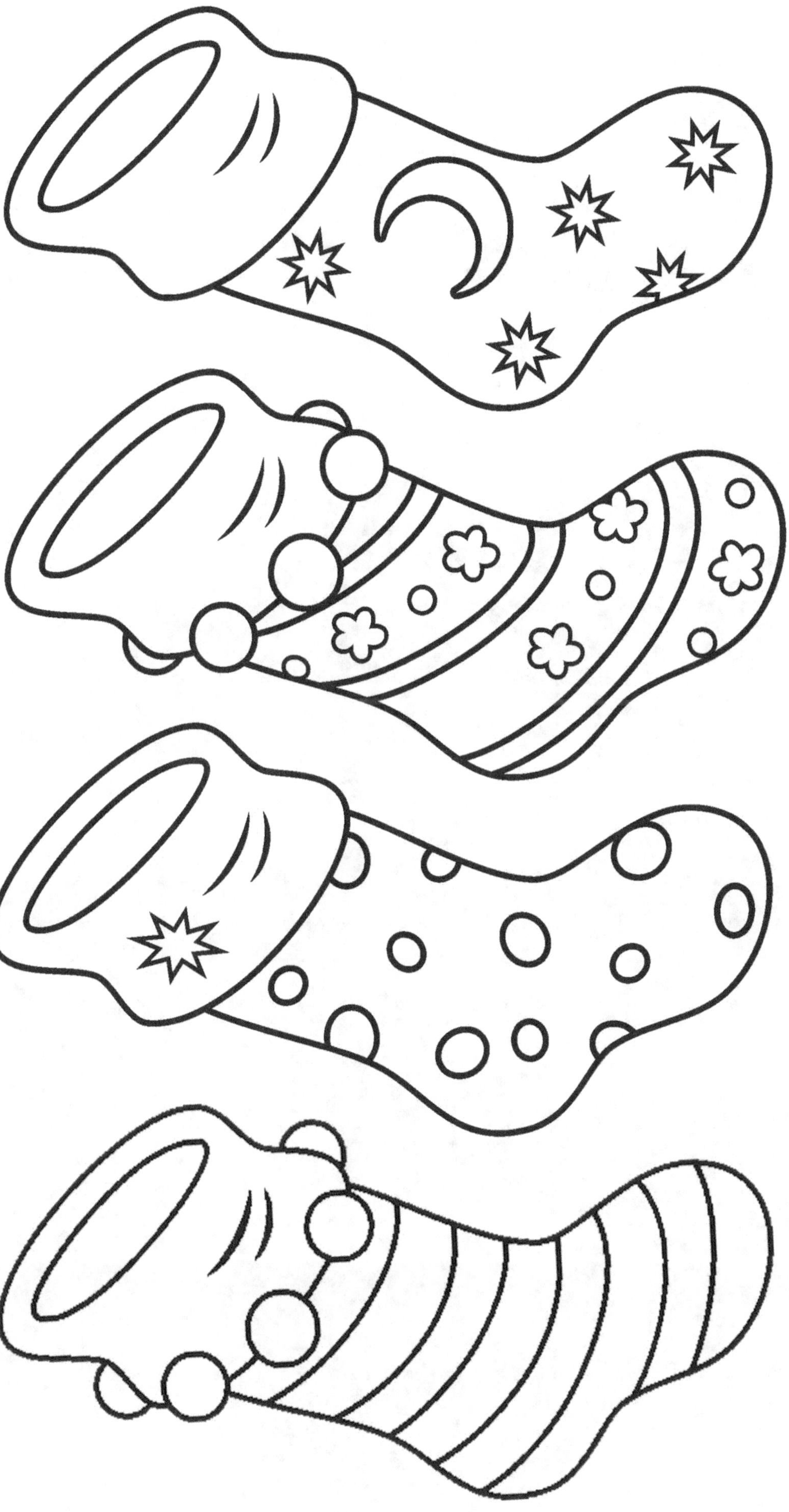

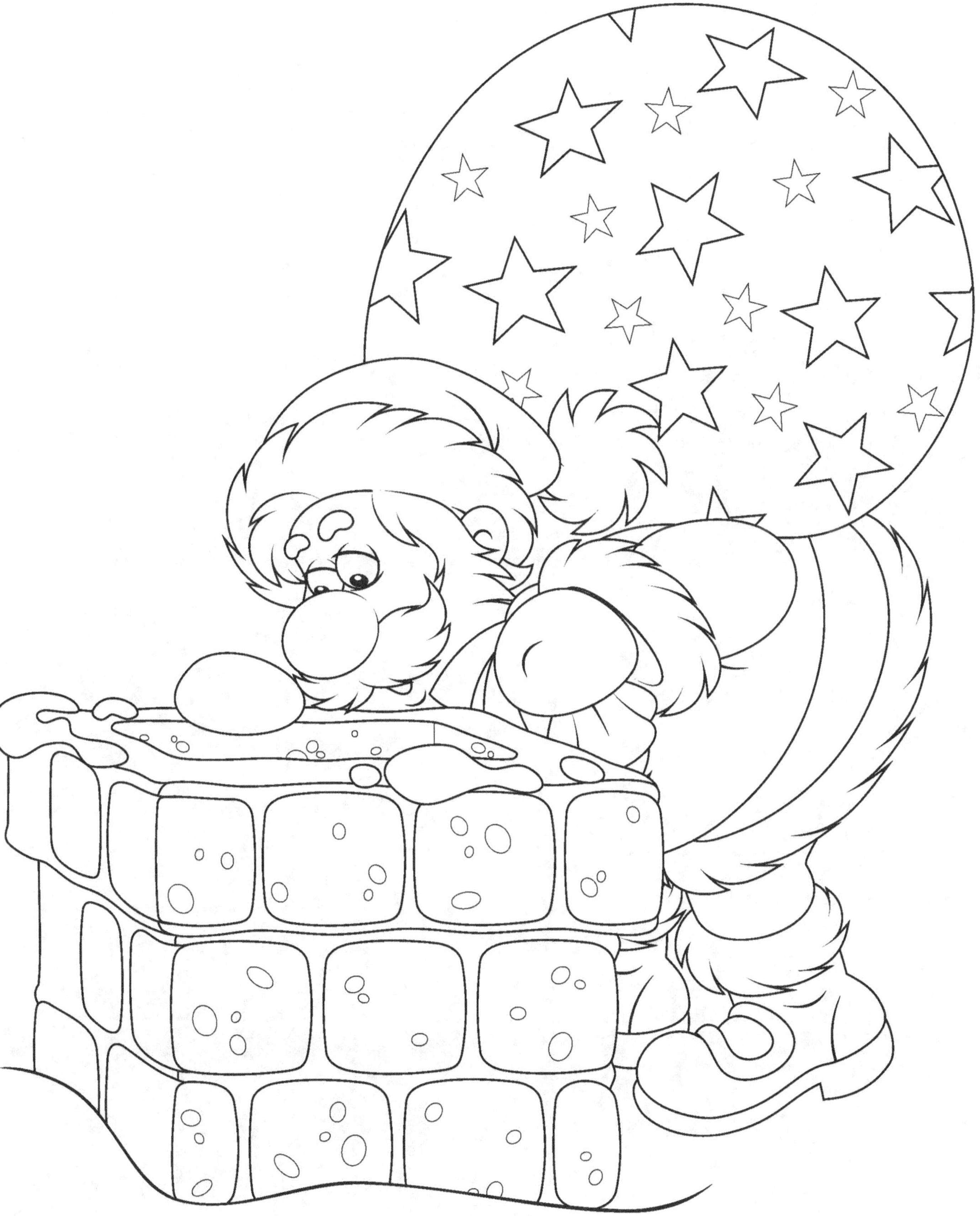

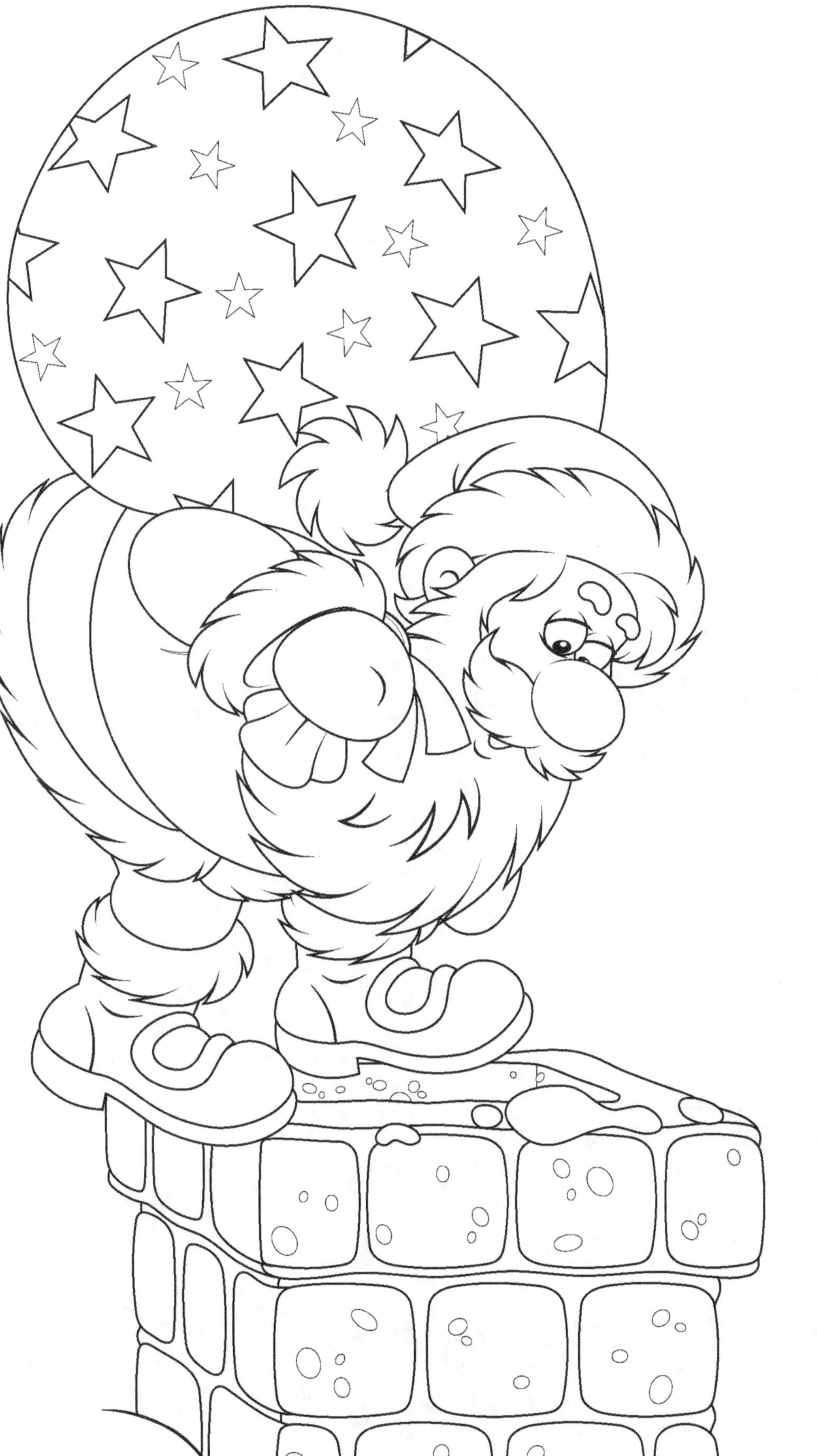

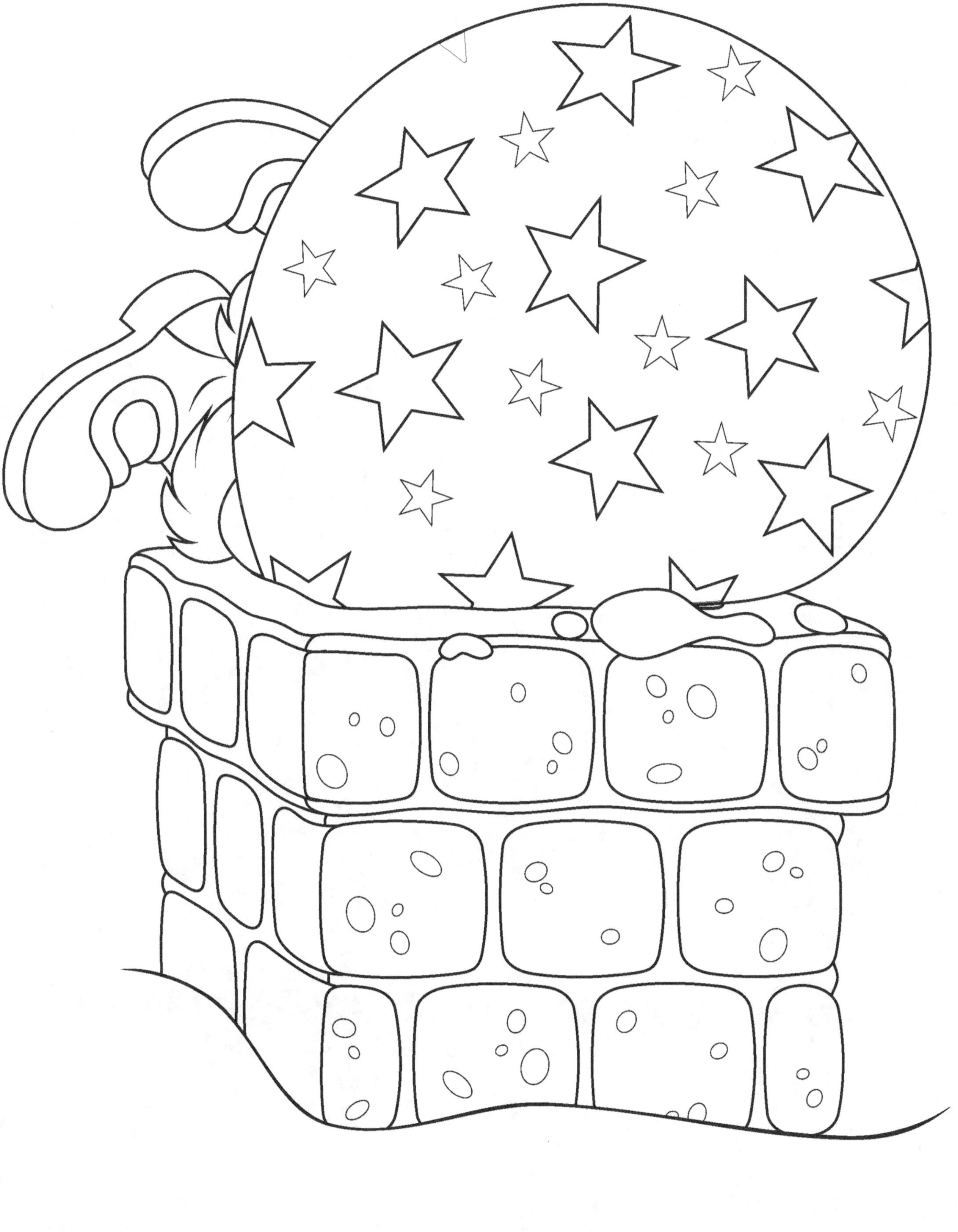

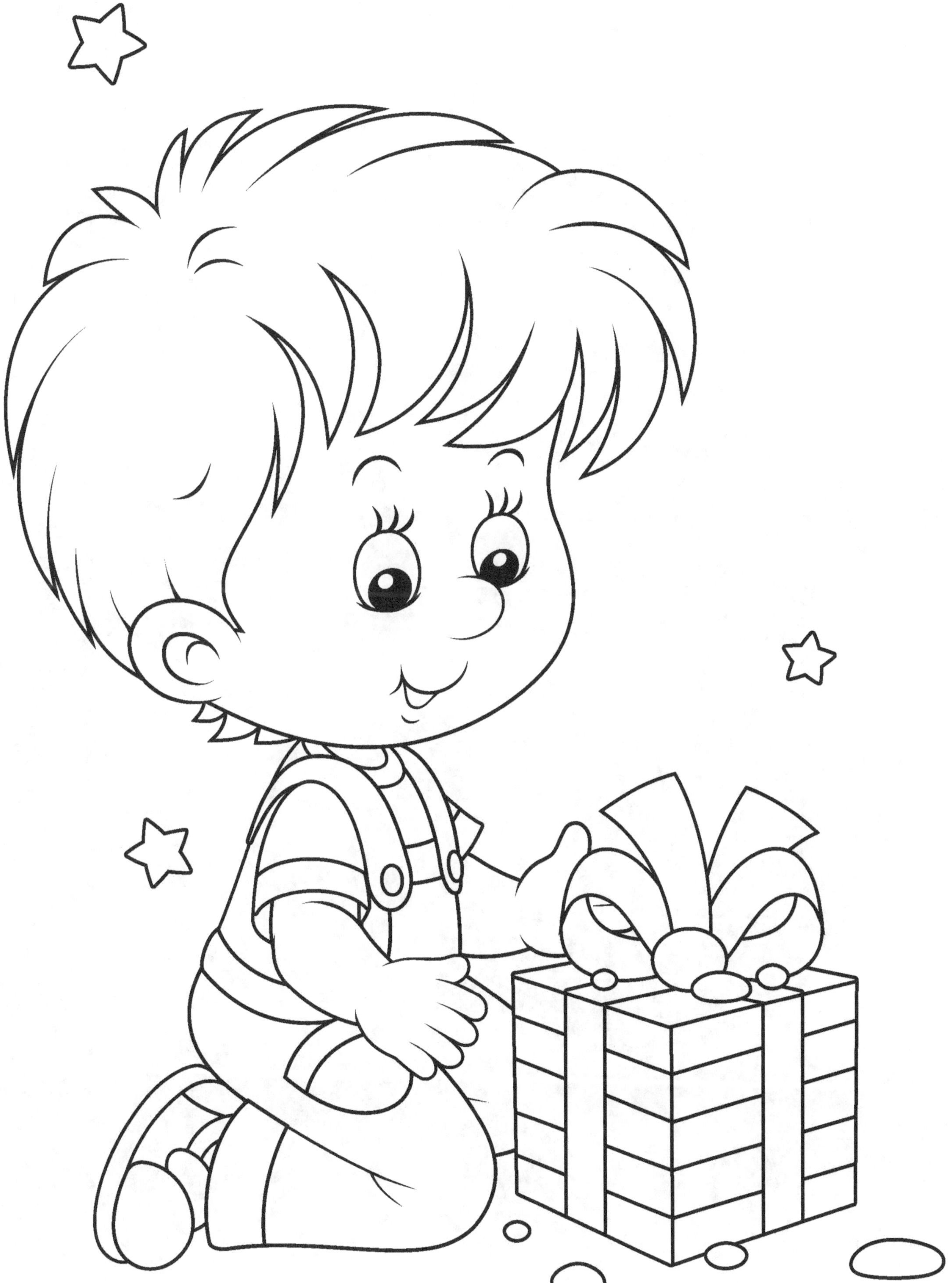

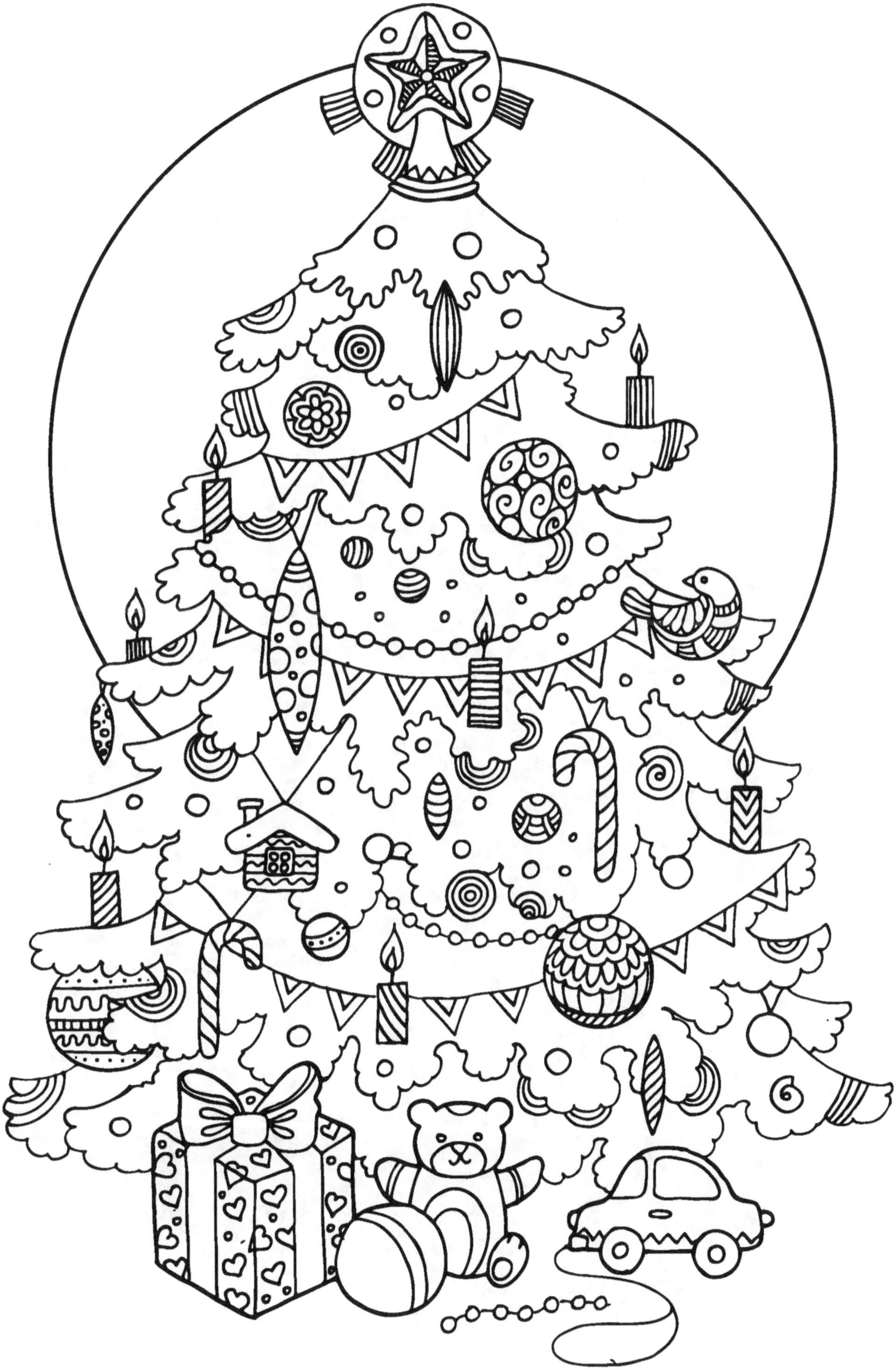

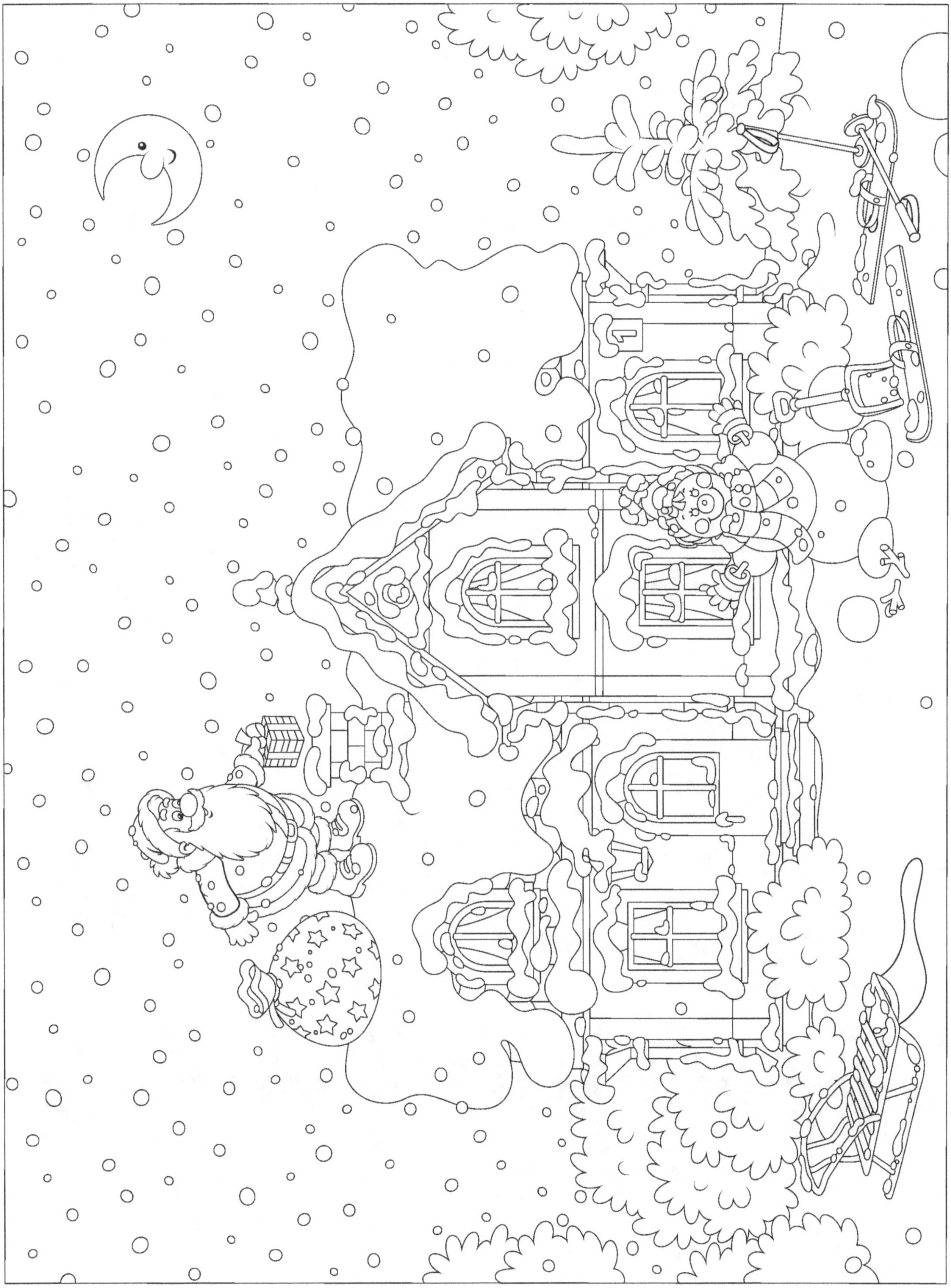

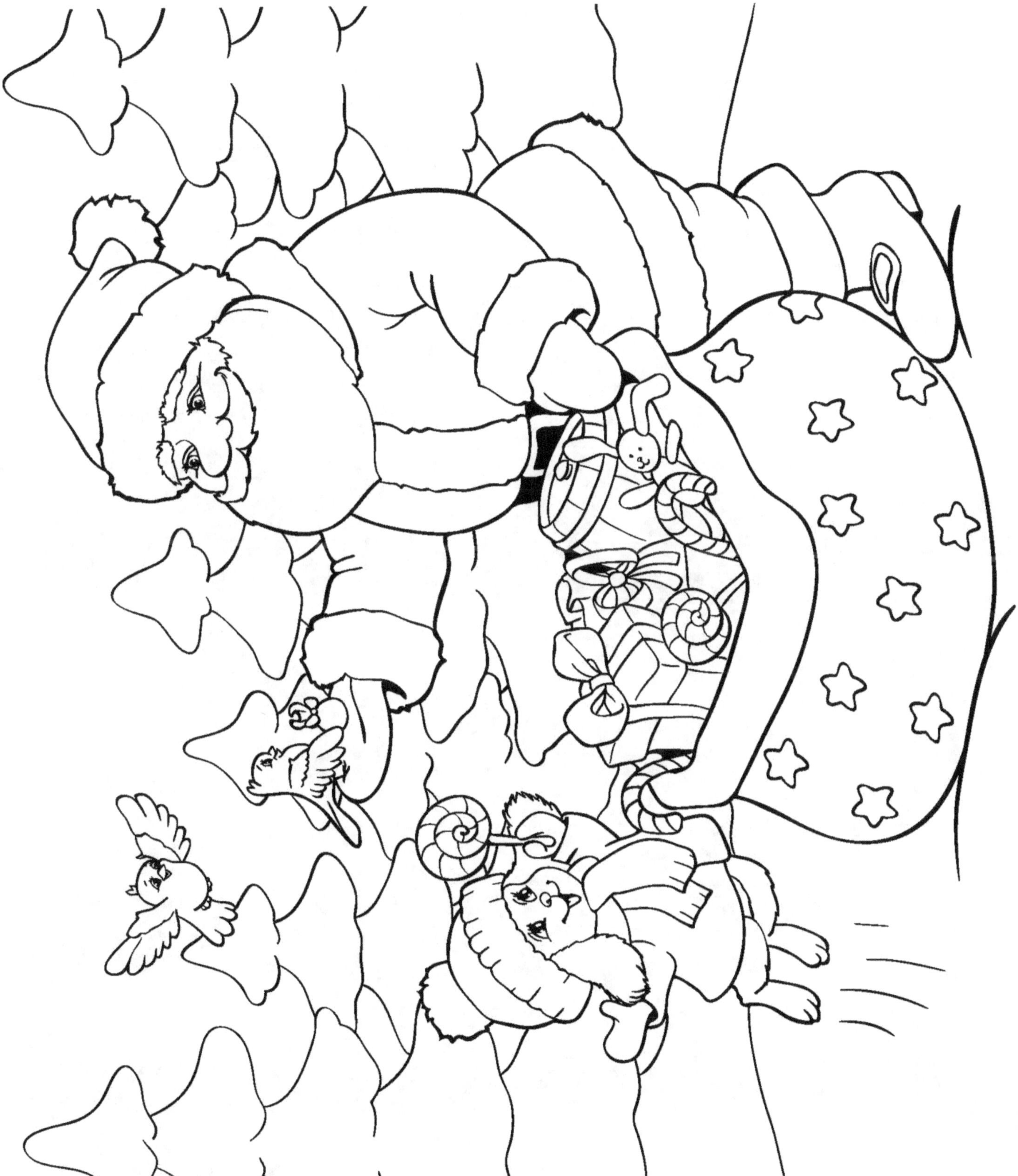

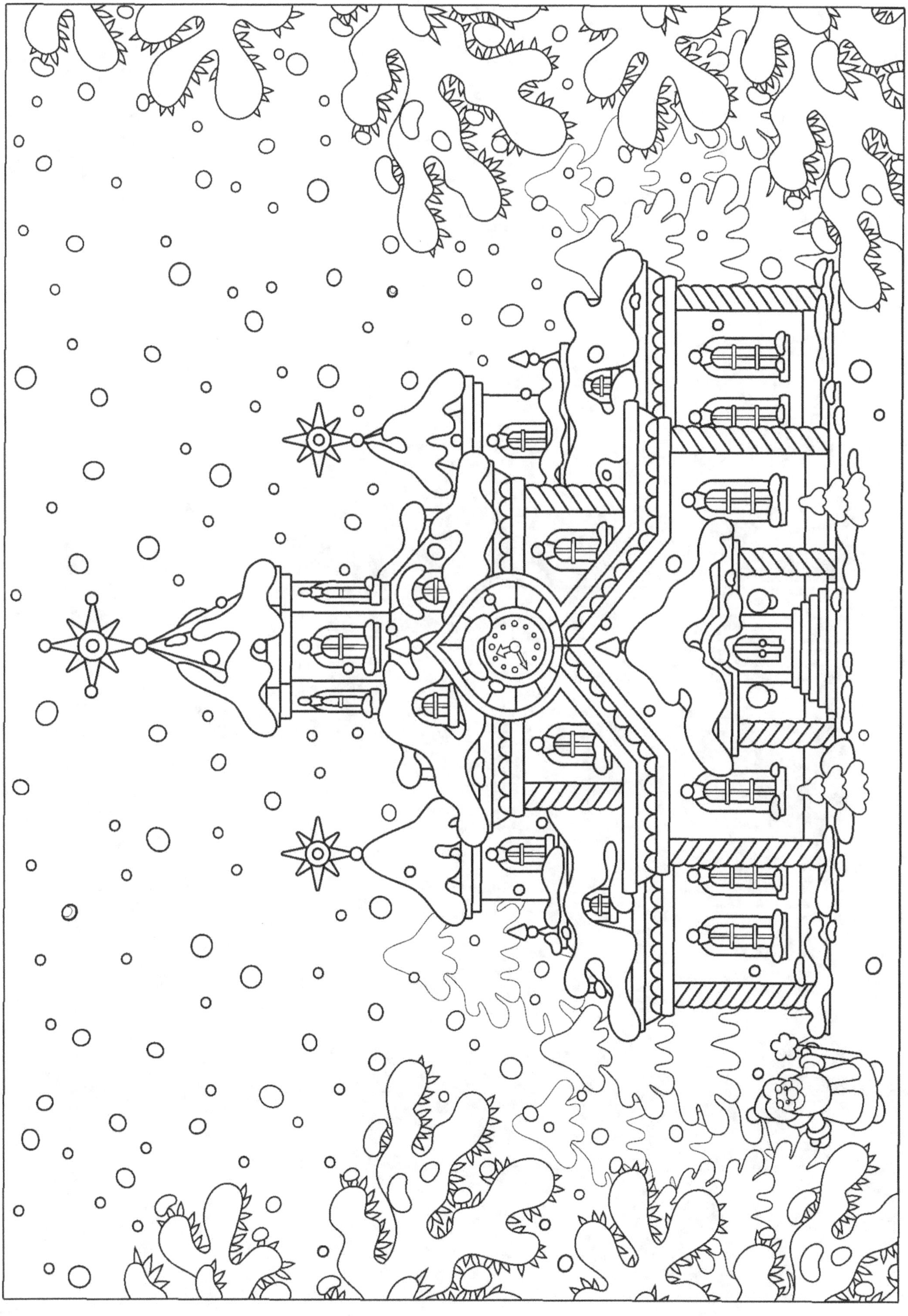

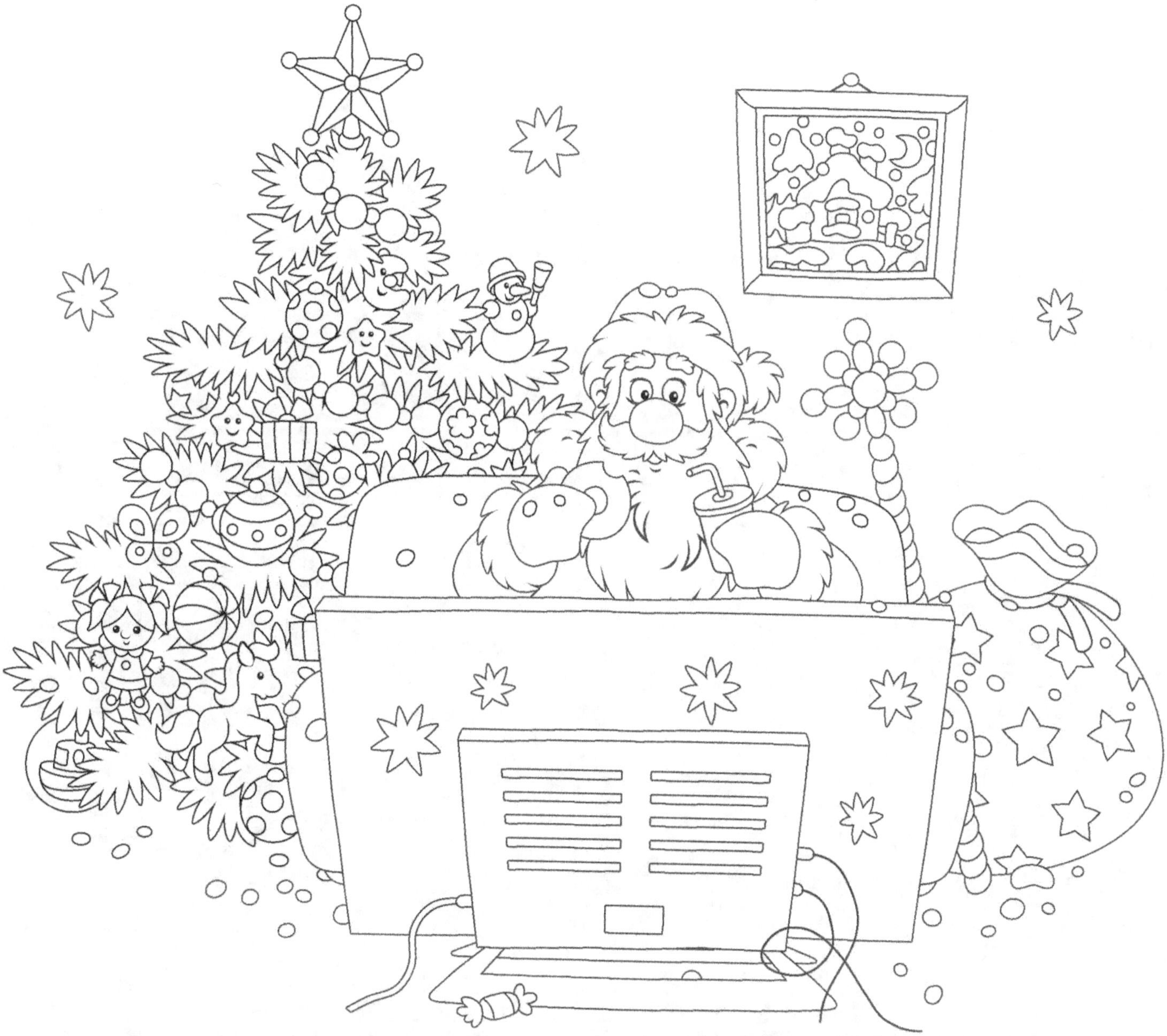

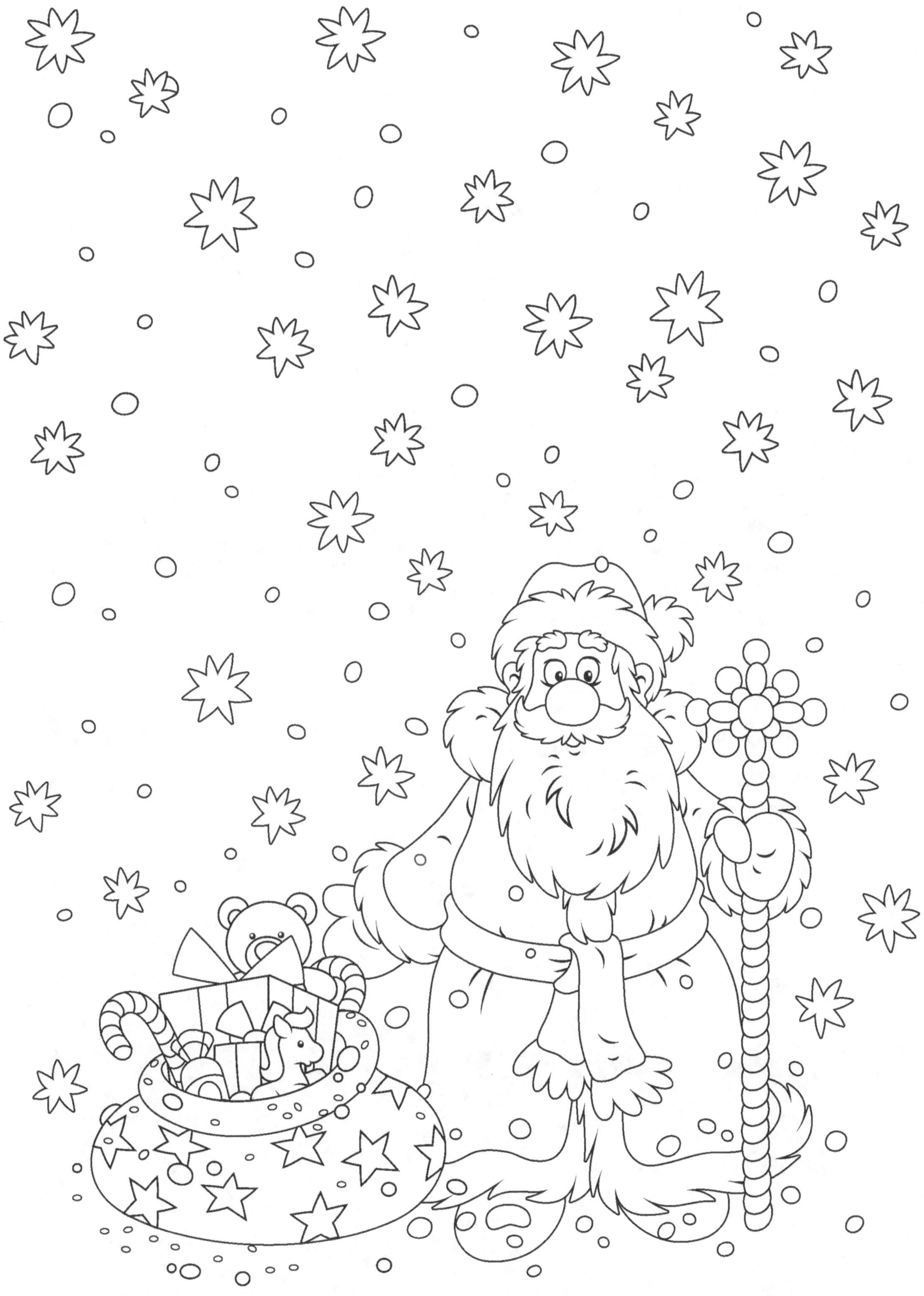

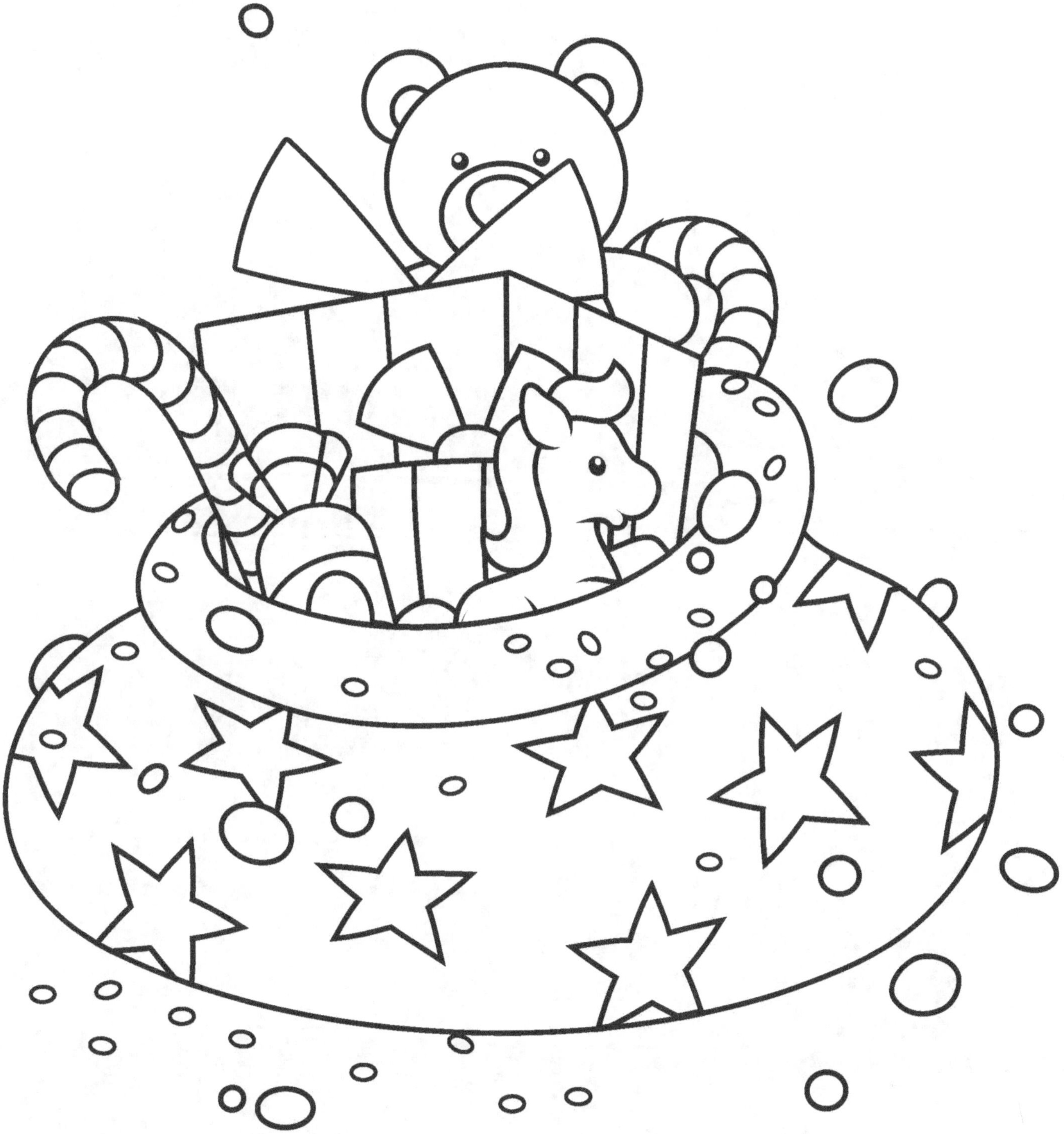

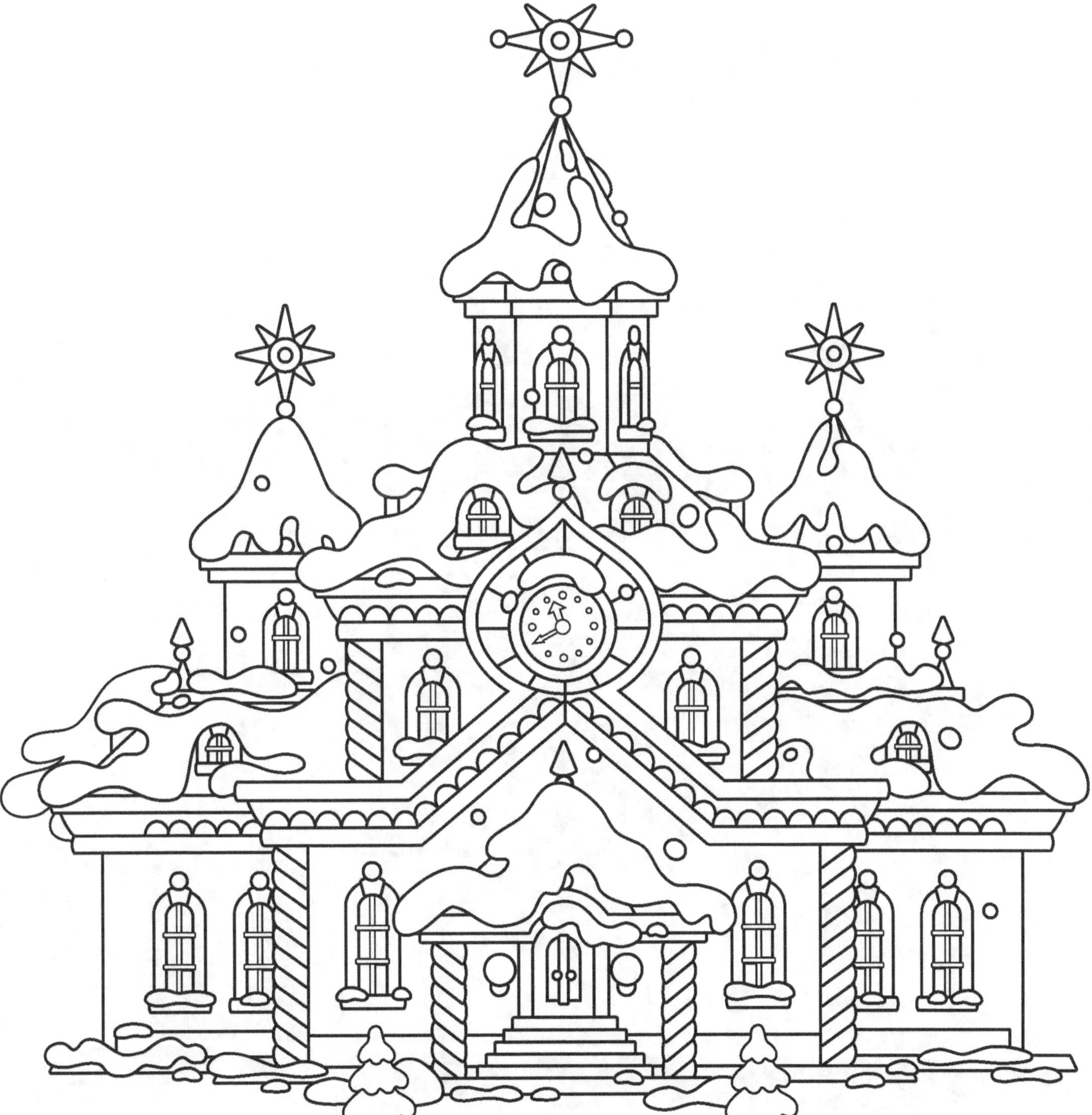

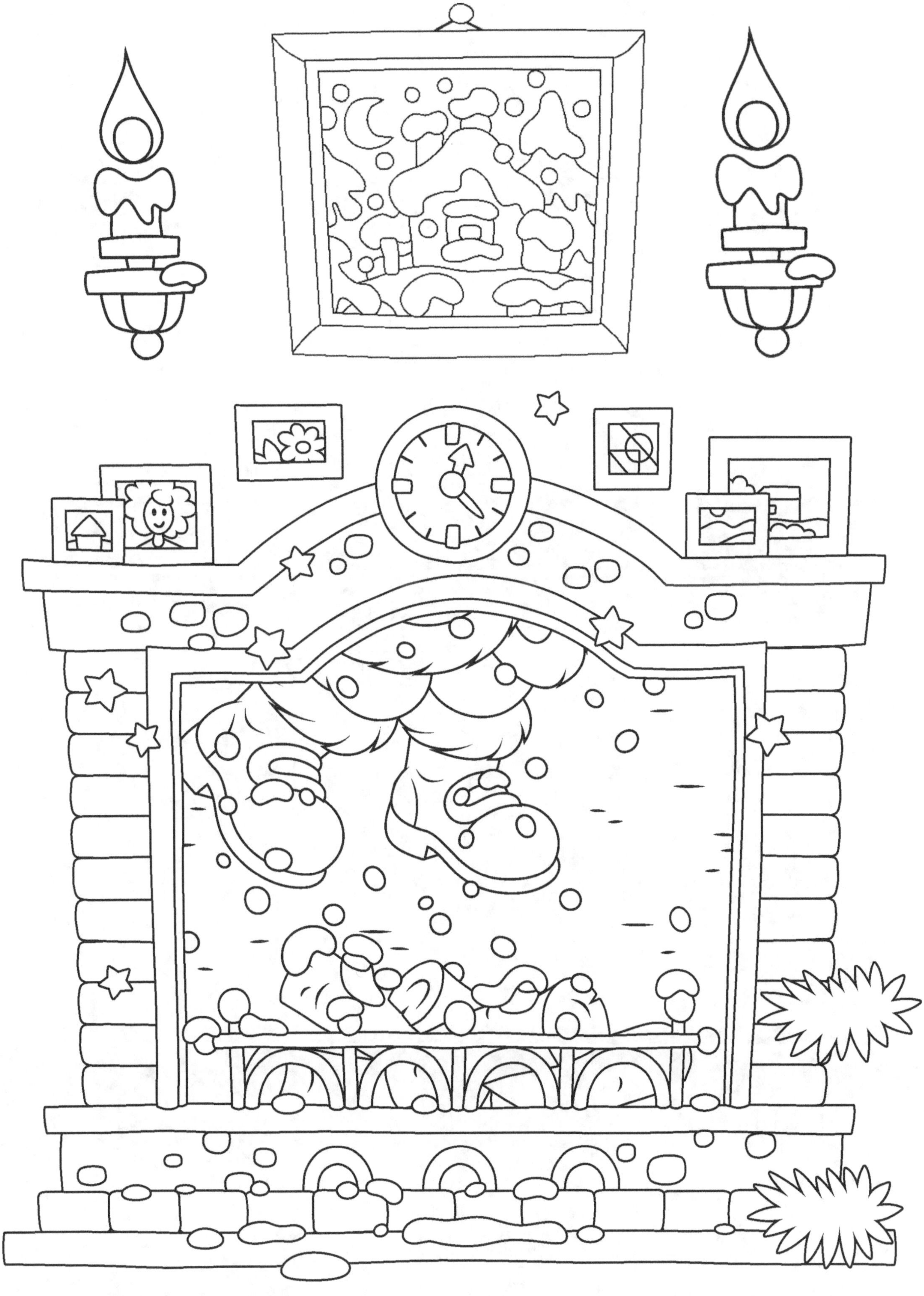

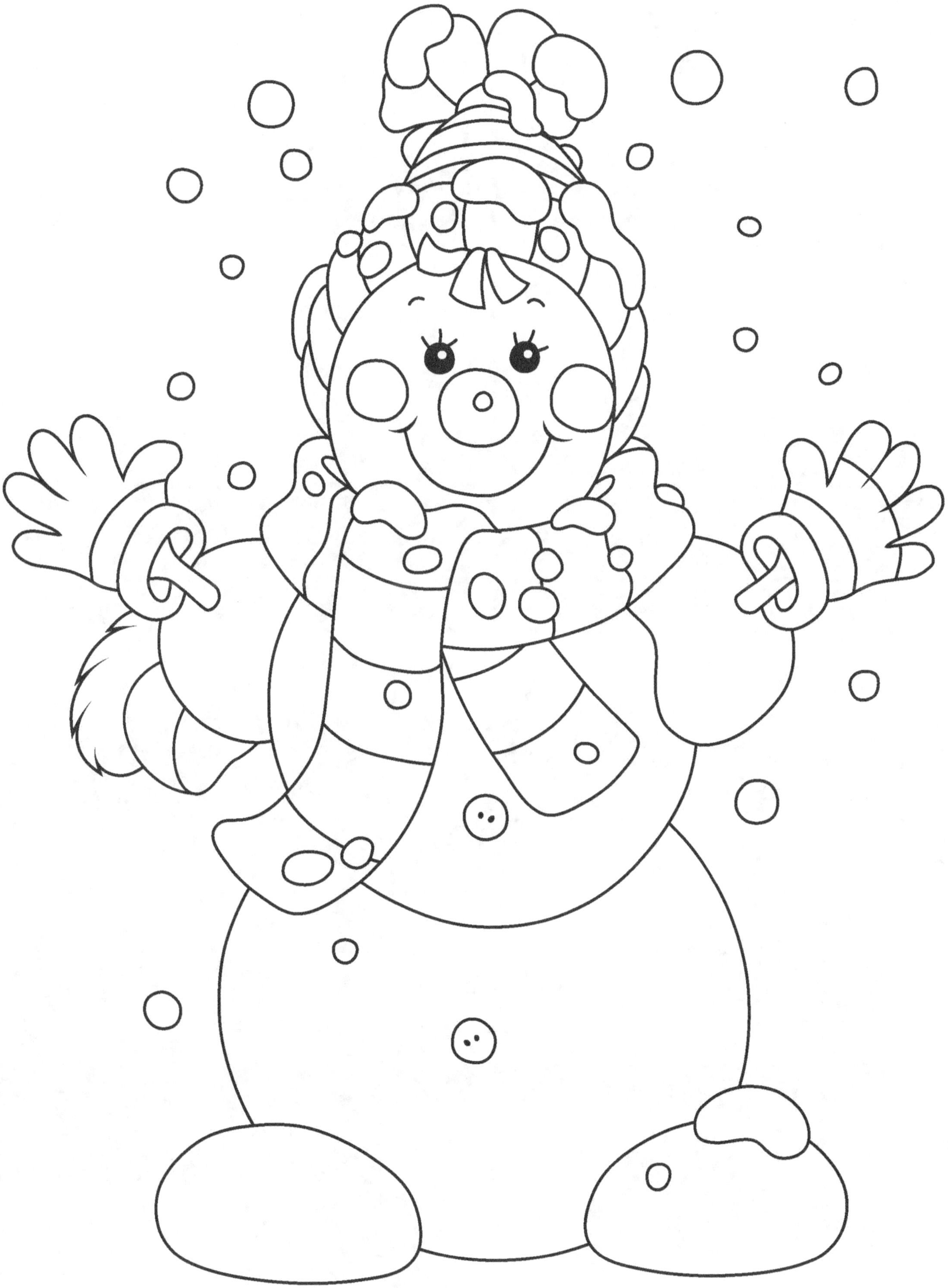

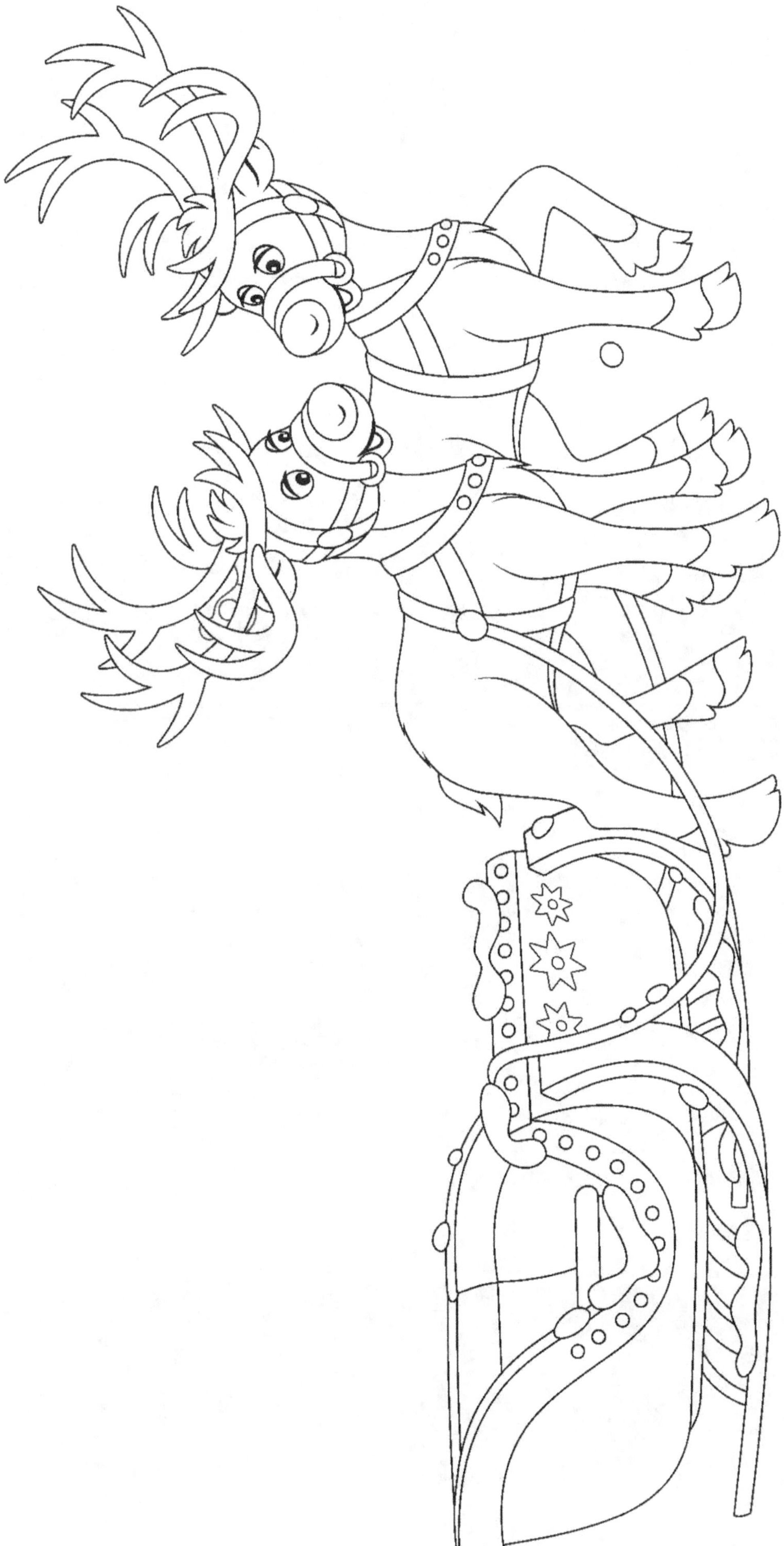

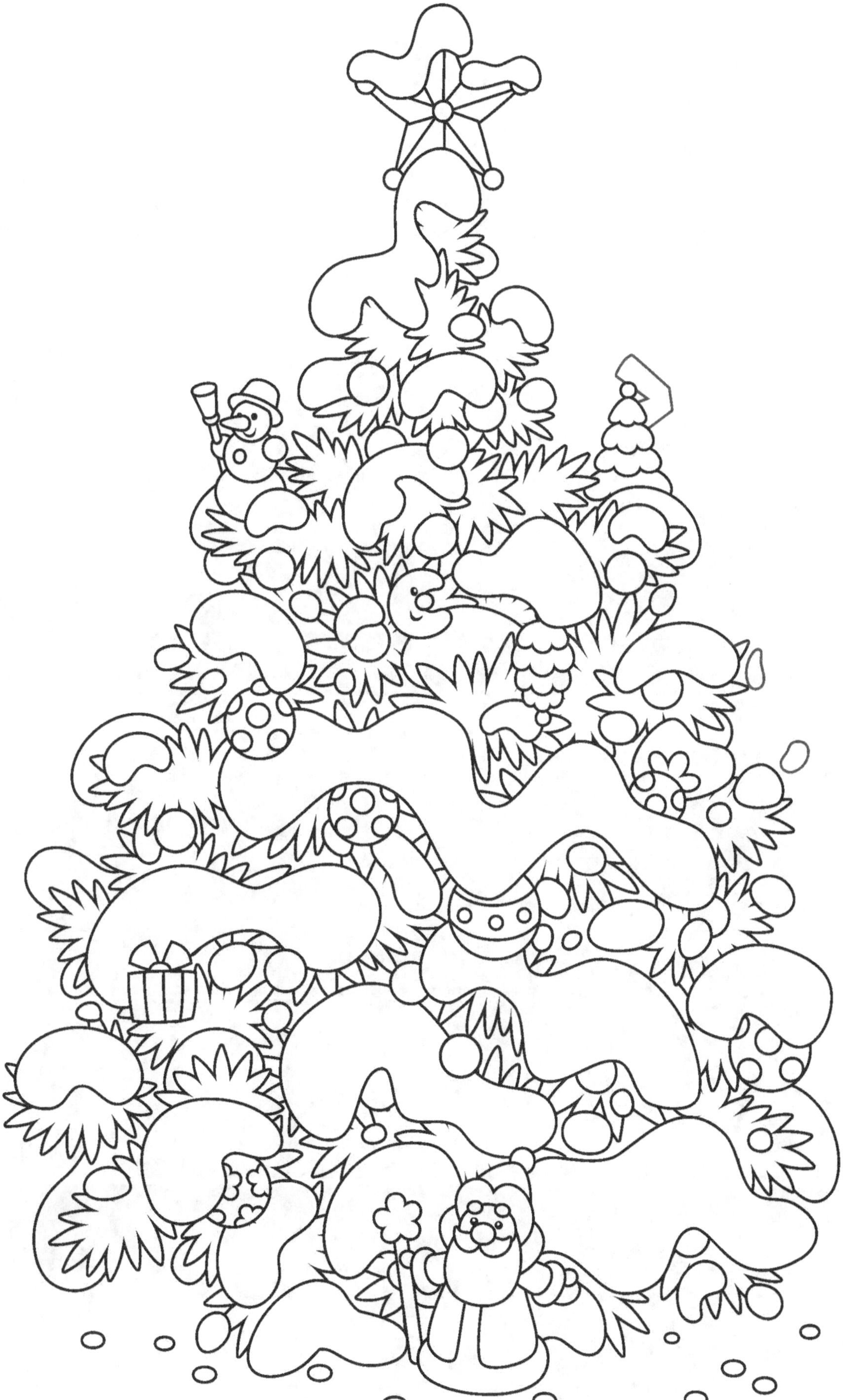

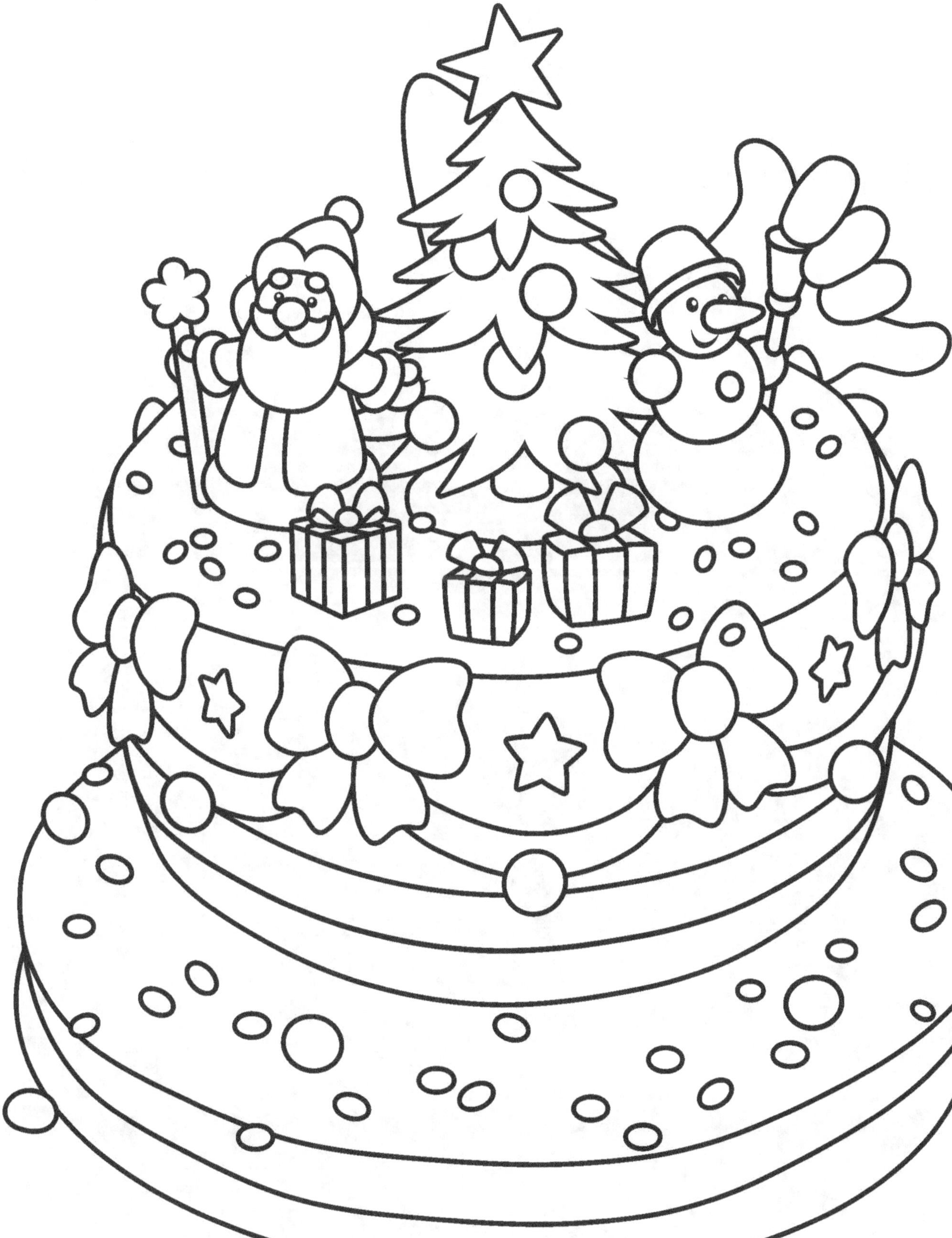

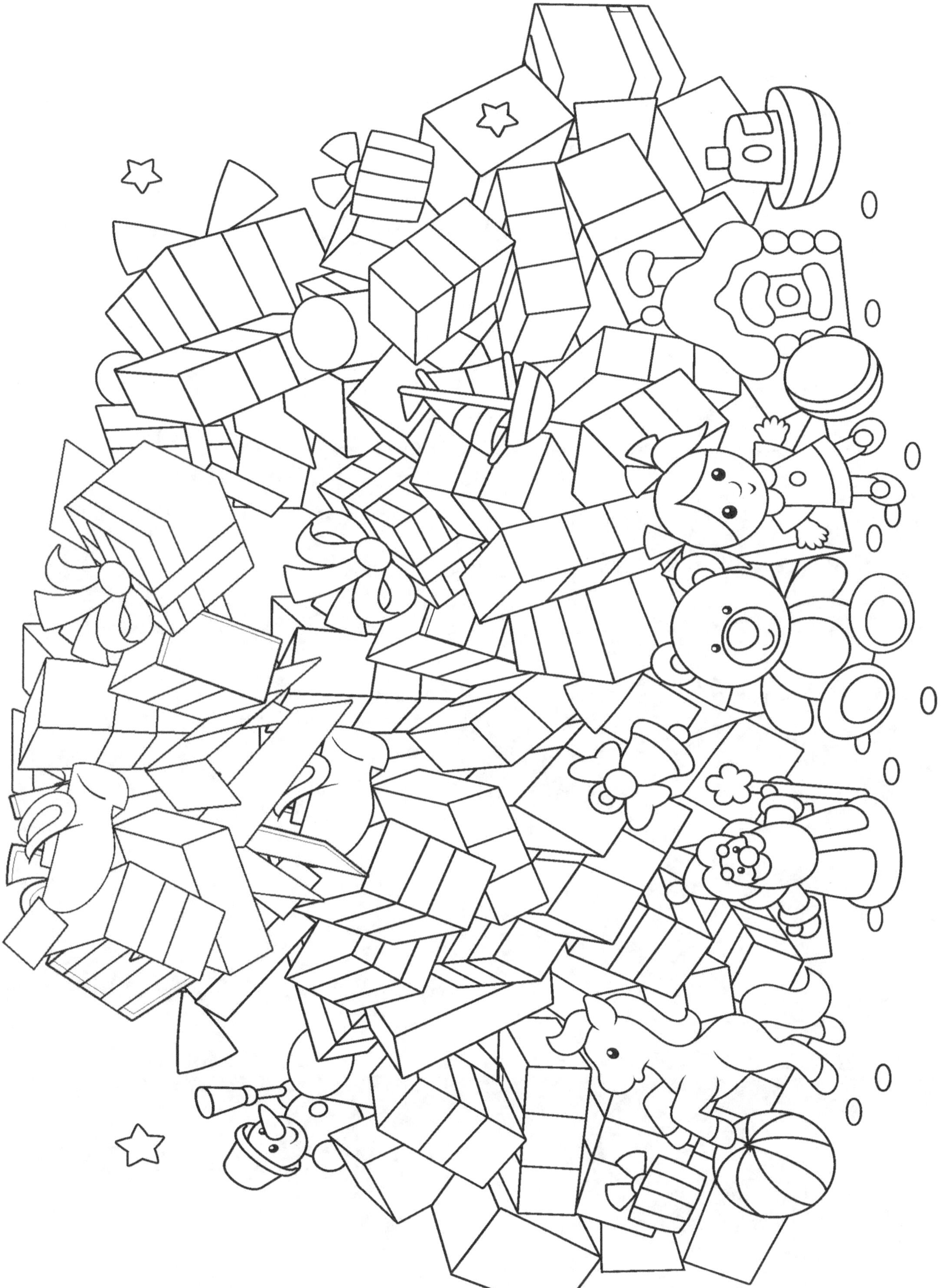

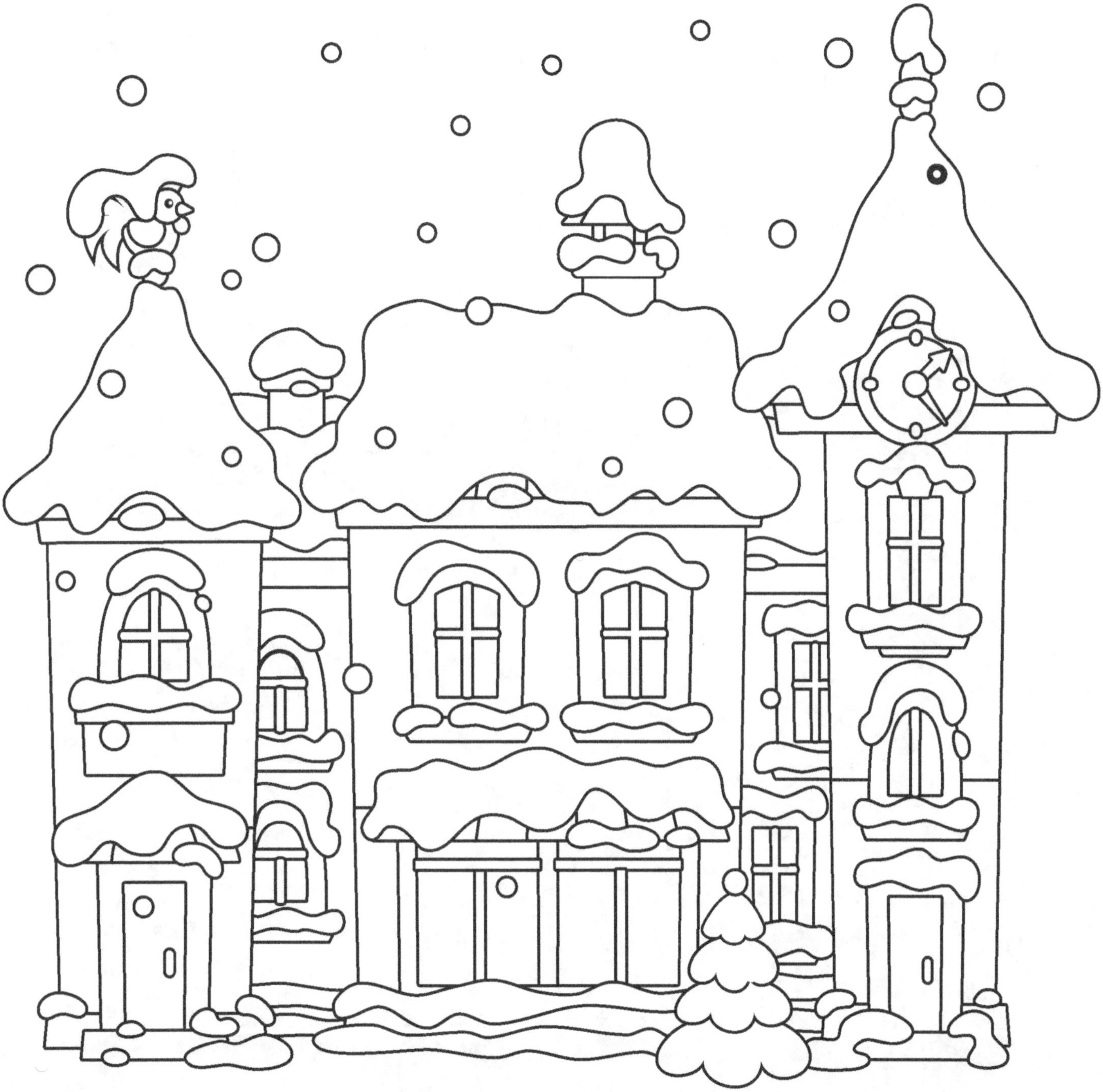

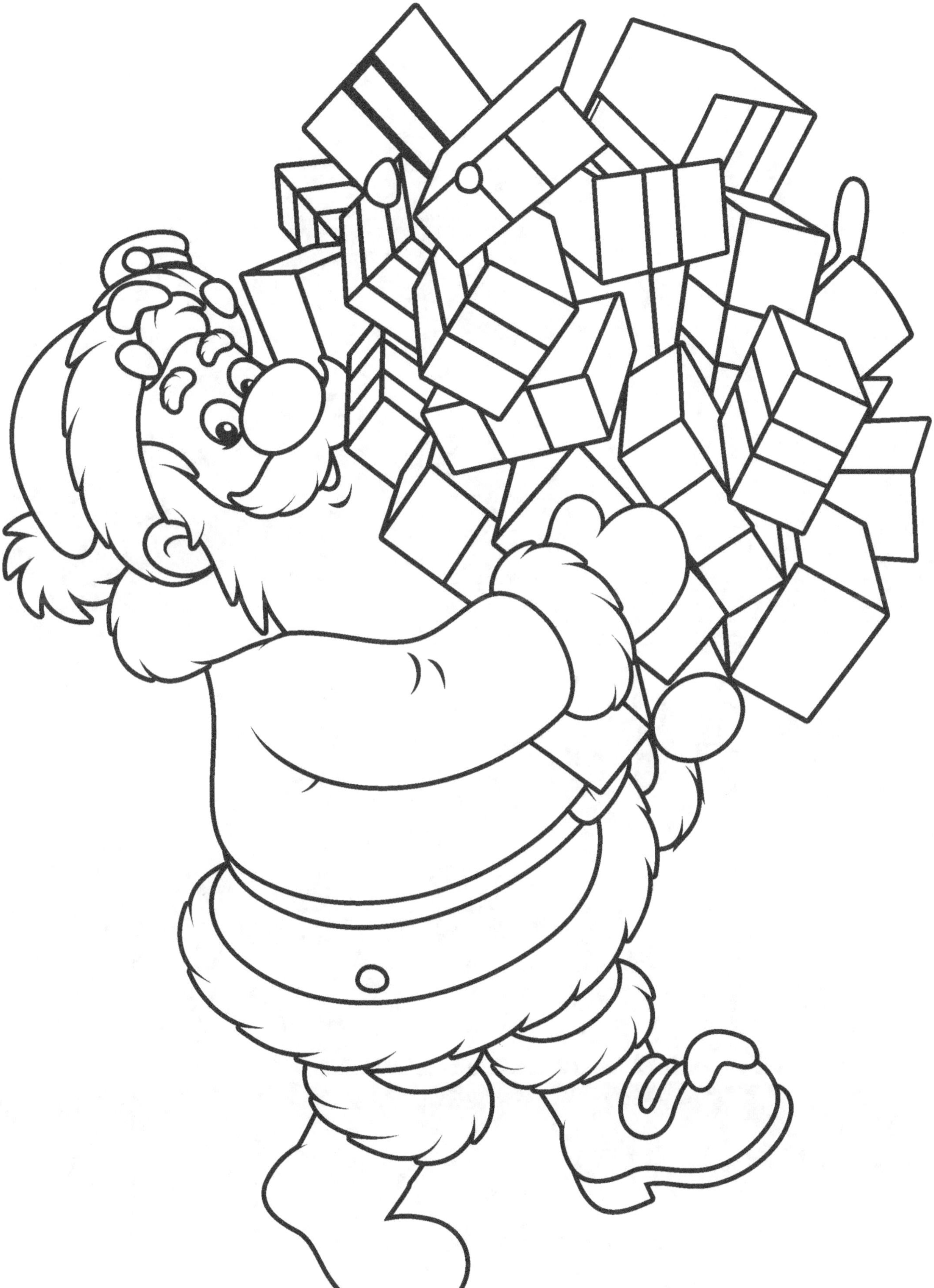

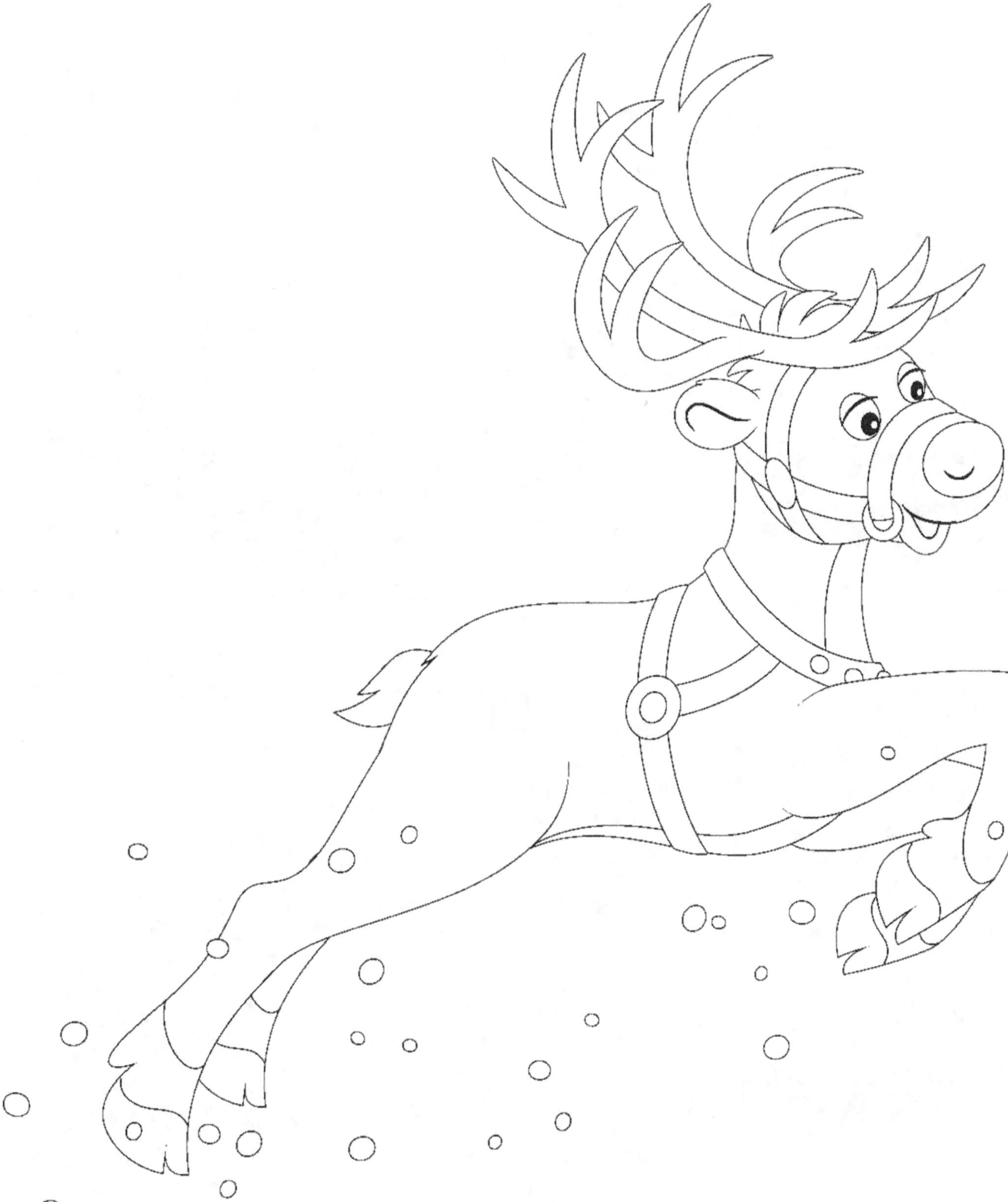

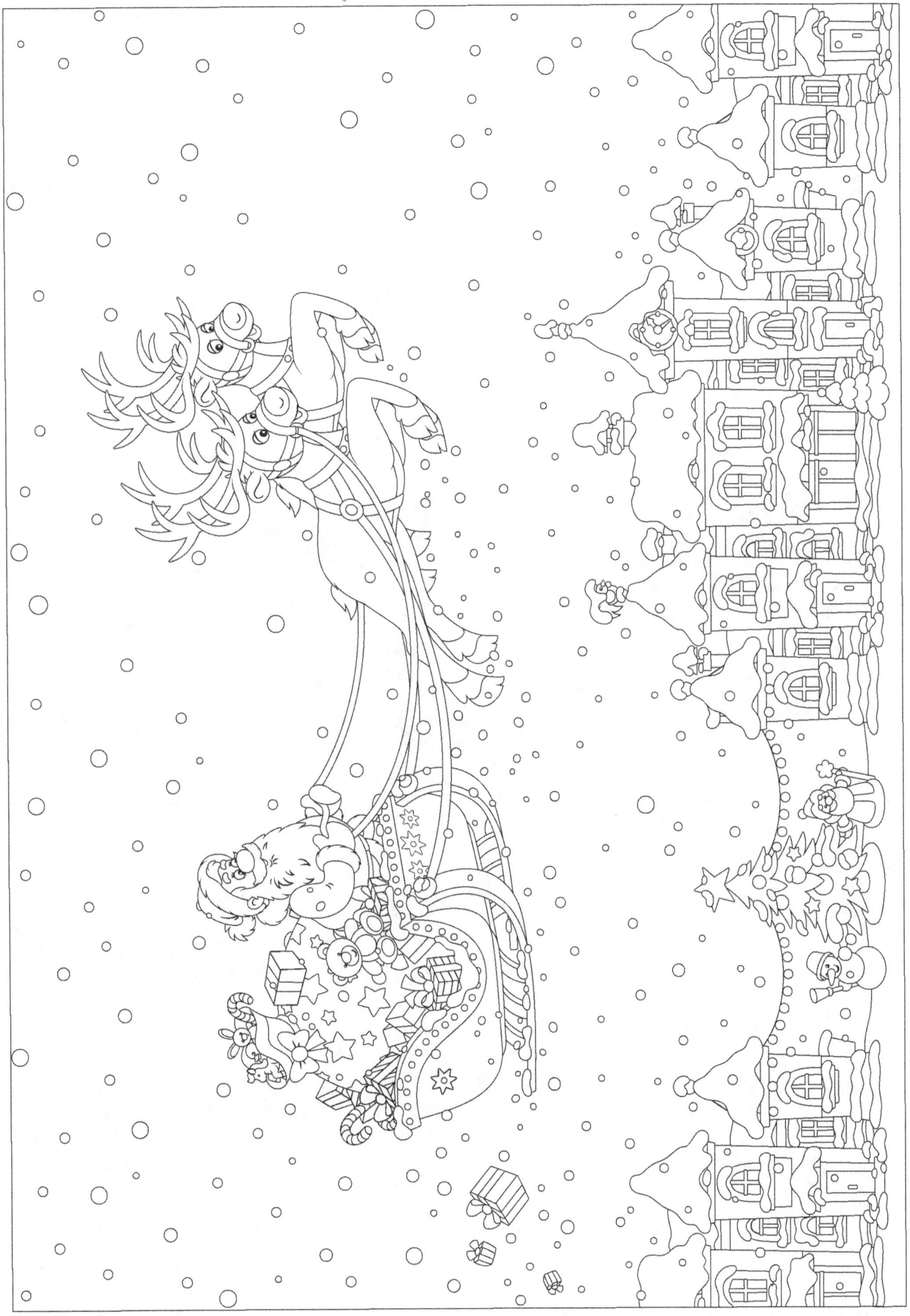

www.ingramcontent.com/pod-product-compliance
Lightning Source LLC
Chambersburg PA
CBHW080939170526
45158CB00008B/2309
* 9 7 8 1 0 8 5 9 7 6 4 2 8 *